AND WHEN WE PRAY

The Prayer Warrior's Weapons of Warfare

Dr. Phyllis Glass

KP PUBLISHING COMPANY

Copyright 2020 by Dr. Phyllis Glass

All rights reserved. In accordance with the U.S. Copyright Act of 1976, the scanning, uploading, and electronic sharing of any part of this book without the permission of the publisher is unlawful piracy and theft of the author's intellectual property. If you would like to use material from this book (other than for review purposes), prior written permission must be obtained by contacting the publisher at info@knowledgepowerinc.com.

Thank you for your support of the author's rights.

ISBN: 978-1-950936-88-5 (Paperback)
ISBN: 978-1-950936-89-2(Ebook)
Library of Congress Control Number: 2020920455

Editor: Stacie Fujii, Frank D. Williams
Cover Design: Juan Roberts, Creative Lunacy
Interior Design: Jennifer Houle
Literary Director: Sandra Slayton James

Unless otherwise noted, Scriptures quotations are taken from the King James version, Holy Bible is in the Public Domain.

Other Scripture quotation are from the following sources: Holy Bible, New Living Translation, copyright 1996, 2004, 2007, 2015 by Tyndale House Foundation. Used by permission of Tyndale House Publishers, Inc. Carol Stream, Illinois 60188. All rights reserved.

Published by:

KP Publishing Company
Publisher of Fiction, Nonfiction & Children's Books
Valencia, CA 91355
www.kp-pub.com

Printed in the United States of America

Dedication

I dedicate this book to:

My Mother, Mildred L. (Grant) Rucker, for the many years of sharing the Word of God, and the importance of going to God in prayer.

My prayer warrior siblings, Yvonda, Edwyna, Edward, Suelyn, and Lisa, whose love, support, and prayers brought us through.

My children, Troy, Rejene, Stacey, Roberto, and Tonya; your lives demonstrate that prayers of the faithful yield results.

My late husband, Dr. Hymie Glass, Sr. (July 11, 1937–April 27, 2018), a dedicated prayer warrior whose love for God and faith in God revealed the destiny we shared as one.

Preface

WHILE THERE ARE several writings on the subject of prayer, I felt compelled to share with the world a life lesson about one of the most profound yet rewarding topic: the prayer warriors' weapons of warfare. I encourage those who desire to start or strengthen their prayer life, to seek through developing their knowledge of The Holy Trinity which is made up of God the Father, God the Son, and God the Holy Spirit. Having that knowledge is key to understanding the ultimate purpose and plan of God.

While other sources as referenced were used, the majority of this book is comprised of an exegesis of scripture taken directly from the King James Version of the Holy Bible. I intend to give clarity to the definition, purpose, and benefits of knowing and appreciating this Almighty God we know, love and serve in a more intimate way. The Holy Bible (sometimes called the Living Word) is being used to describe each person of the Trinity. You will find the contents of this book will actually come alive as you discover all the attributes of each person of the Trinity. My personal experiences with each person of the trinity have been profound throughout my life journey. It was only through my belief and faith in God, my relationship with Jesus Christ, and the Holy Spirit that caused me to be aware of the assignment of my gifts and how they are used.

In brief, I was given beforehand, the knowledge of events such as the disaster of the Air Florida Flight 90 in 1982, that hit the bridge and went into the Potomac river; the horrific crash of PanAm Flight 103 in 1988 in which over 300 lives were lost; the great earthquake named Izmit, of Rocael Golcuk which lies in the northeastern part of Turkey, where over 17,000 people lost their lives and hundred more were injured.

Because I had received knowledge from God before each actual event, I was frustrated but continued with my search to find out what could I have done. I asked God in prayer to reveal why I was given these dreams and visions as most of them seemed to portend tragic events. One of the many significant dreams that came to me involved a friend who I will discuss later. I was desperate to find my purpose, and how or even if my prayer life could possibly affect others.

I want you to adhere to 2 Timothy 2:15 which says, "Study to show thyself approved unto God; a workman that needeth not to be ashamed, rightly dividing the word of truth." It means to seek out on your own those truths that coincide with the infallible Word of God. My desire also is for you to maintain your concentration and interest in the subject matter. Only a select number of scriptures are being referenced which will cause you to put in the work that will bring you the reward of knowing you've made progress. It will enable you to see what each person of the Trinity means to you and how they have impacted your personal experiences. There are many benefits and rewards that come with the revelation knowledge you are able to uncover on their own. Utilizing this method, I believe will give you more structure as you embark on a magnificent journey to becoming the anointed prayer warrior God intended you to be.

Foreword

FOR A FEW years now, I have been privileged to be called "Pastor" by Dr. Phyllis Glass. A host of our church community have experienced the grace, patience and faith of Dr. Glass. She has modeled for others her faith in God's absolute faithfulness which, ultimately, is the only real certainty that any of us have when we pray.

Through decades of personal experience, Dr. Glass has proven these practical and biblical principles shared in her book. She makes it clear that we are all called of God to be Prayer Participants in His kingdom.

This book proves that we are surrounded by opportunities to impact our world through this powerful means of prayer. Filled with challenging teaching and spiced with remarkable real-life stories, this book equips those who are beginning in prayer to those who are mature prayer partners. This book illuminates the truth that the power of God is available to those who listen to His voice and obey what He says, so that His power is made available on behalf of others.

The Prayer Warrior's Weapons of Warfare spells out the tools to use in prayer. The benefits, experiences and testimonials throughout the book will revolutionize your prayer life. Whether you are a beginner

AND WHEN WE PRAY

or an advanced prayer warrior this book has a wealth of knowledge to add to your arsenal. You are stepping into the pages of a book that is born out of years of fruitful experience.

God has made it clear from Genesis to Revelation that the believer's prayer is the match that lights the fuse to release explosive power into the affairs of men.

Our ultimate resource for knowledge on the subject of prayer must be the Word of God as we prepare for spiritual combat.

God is calling out a vast army of His people to pray, and they are saying, "Show me how!" I have found no better training manual than this book. It explains what prayer is, what it does, what different kinds of prayer look like, how to hear from God as you pray, the essentials of spiritual warfare and more.

Reading and applying the principles of *The Prayer Warrior's Weapons of Warfare* has all the potential to upgrade your prayer ministry and impact your community decisively for the Kingdom of God.

It is our pleasure to introduce you to the book, *The Prayer Warrior's Weapon of Warfare*.

PASTORS FRED & LINDA HODGE
LIVING PRAISE CHRISTIAN CHURCH
PALMDALE & NORTH HOLLYWOOD, CALIFORNIA

Contents

Dedication	*v*
Preface	*vii*
Foreword	*ix*
Introduction	*xii*
CHAPTER 1: The Meaning and Purpose of Prayer	**1**
Definition and Meaning of Prayer	1
The Purpose of Prayer	2
What Makes Prayer Effective?	2
Prayer And The Holy Trinity	7
Elements That Apply To The Lord's Prayer	9
Prayer Should Be Specific	10
Who Are We Praying To?	12
Who's Will Do We Obey?	14
CHAPTER 2: The Importance of Prayer	**15**
Does God Hear Our Prayer?	15
Are Christians Required to Pray?	16
Free Moral Agents	18
The Importance of Prayer	21
When We Should Pray?	25
The Benefits of Prayer	29

CHAPTER 3: Praying in the Spirit — 33
- Are We Required To Pray In The Spirit? — 33
- Praying in the Spirit — 34
- Benefits of Praying in the Spirit — 35
- Gifts of the Spirit — 35

CHAPTER 4: Secrets to Answered Prayer — 39
- Secrets to Answered Prayer — 39
- Conditions of Answered Prayer — 44
- Fasting and Prayer — 46
- Why Are Some Prayers Not Answered? — 50
- Does God Have Limits? — 55

CHAPTER 5: Tools to Use in Battle — 57
- Lessons on Prayer — 57
- Most Effective Bible Verses for Prayer — 58
- Weapons of Warfare — 62
- Fruit of the Spirit — 67

CHAPTER 6: Prayers is Personal — 73
- There's Personality in Prayer — 73
- What Can Prayer Accomplish? — 77
- Prayers that Jesus Prayed — 80

TESTIMONIALS FROM PRAYER WARRIORS — 85
CONCLUSION — 99
- *About the Author* — *101*
- *Acknowledgments* — *103*
- *Bibliography* — *105*

Introduction

THERE ARE HISTORICAL reasons why this book is so important to me. It is not about dreams and/or the interpretation of dreams but is in part about some of the experiences I've had with dreams that caused me to be concerned with prayer and how to apply the weapons of warfare as tools in this fight. I am sharing some of those dreams and why prayer has become critically important for my comfort and spiritual well being; and why prayer was used as a tool or weapon of warfare to make a change when and wherever I could.

My personal experience with each person of the trinity has been profound throughout my journey through life. It was only through my belief and faith in God, my relationship with Jesus Christ, and the Holy Spirit caused me to be aware of the assignment of gifts and how they are used. In brief, I was given beforehand the knowledge of events such as the crash of PanAm Flight 103 in 1988; the disaster of the Air Florida Flight #90 in 1982 that hit the bridge and went into the Potomac River; in 1999, the horrific earthquake named Izmit, Rocael Golcuk which lies in the northeastern part of Turkey, in which over 17,000 people lost their lives and several more were injured. Some of those dreams have included family members where I've been able to share with those affected.

AND WHEN WE PRAY

While those three major tragic events were revealed to me prior to each incident in a combination of dreams, they were not the only catalyst to changing my prayer life. In early 1974, and prior to the three aforementioned events above, one of my sisters who lived in Omaha, Nebraska at the time, called me and asked me if I remembered someone I used to work with. This person and I were good friends while we were employed at a drive-up restaurant there in Omaha. We became disconnected after I moved from Omaha to California in the mid 1960's and did not stay in touch. It started with these dreams in which I was trying to get my children out of the house and safe from a fire somewhere on the horizon. There was a series of three dreams within a three-week period of time. In one dream, I found myself in a panic as I tried to push my children out of a bedroom window; in another dream I found myself along with someone else watering the roof with a garden hose to keep the fire from spreading; and yet another dream I again found myself in panic as I attempted to usher my kids out of the house to save them.

Shortly after that series of dreams, I was getting ready for work. I went to the kitchen to turn the fire under a pot to melt the Crisco shortening I had used to fry chicken the night before. I was going to melt it down, then transfer it to a used coffee container to cool and store. I forgot it was on the stove when I went to take a shower. As I rushed back to the kitchen, when I pulled the lid off, flames shot to the ceiling. I was not well versed in putting out a grease fire, as the garden hose was not the answer. That effort resulted in a larger fire that spread to the kitchen cabinets on each side of the stove. The fire department was very prompt in their arrival to contain the fire. The children were already in the process of leaving for school and not affected. I thought to myself, "wow" my dreams must have been some kind of divine warning.

I was heartbroken when I realized the kitchen fire was not the only thing I should have been worried about. The call from the sister in

Introduction

Omaha was devastating. My friend who had married lost three children 8, 7 and 3 years old in a terrible duplex fire. It was then I felt a relentless need to figure out what if anything I could have done that could have made a difference in that tragedy. I was feeling a heavy burden to do something but was at a loss at what it was that I should do. I went to my pastor, Rev. Dr. Johnnie Brown of St. Timothy Community Church, San Bernardino. I talked to him about the dream and my friend's loss and asked what I could have done. I told him that dream was just one of several I'd had in times past. We discussed the gifts of the Spirit, more specifically, the revelation gifts. Dr. Brown called to my remembrance biblical accounts of the "prophets of old" often referred to as prophets of doom. I was not happy with that gift. At that time, I did not have a clear understanding of the importance of "gifts of the Spirit," or what my responsibility should be with this God-given gift.

That event where my friend lost her children, was definitely one that caused me to question my purpose, my walk with God, my personal relationship with Christ and my responsibility to the Holy Spirit. In times past, there were many events that I was aware of, but some was dismissed as "déjà vu" or have I been there before? type of incidents. My focus was quite different as I made a commitment to grow in my Christian walk where I felt I had the liberty to share; and prayed where I felt prayer was the only answer. Even when I was unsure of whether my prayer would have an impact on anyone else, I discovered overall, my prayer had worth and value.

Hebrews 11:6 tells us,

> *"But without faith, it is impossible to please Him: of he that cometh to God must believe that He is, and that He is a rewarder of them that diligently seek Him.*

AND WHEN WE PRAY

In Genesis 18:23 and 19:29, Abraham prayed for God to save the cities of Sodom and Gomorrah. He asked, "Would you destroy even the righteous along with the wicked?" Abraham prayed and bargained with God but was only able to see Him spare a small remnant to include his nephew Lot. And so, I determined that my prayers may or may not have the ability to save or help someone. But I knew my response should conform to God's will for myself and those God has charged me to pray for.

CHAPTER 1

The Meaning and Purpose of Prayer

Definition and Meaning of Prayer

According to *Merriam-Webster*[1] dictionary, prayer is defined as "an address (such as a petition) to God or a god in word or thought; a set order of words used in praying; an earnest request or wish."

The *Oxford Dictionary*[2] defines prayer as "a solemn request for help or expression of thanks addressed to God or another deity. Examples include: (Prayers) A religious service, especially a regular one, at which people gather in order to pray together. '500 people were detained as they attended Friday prayers.'

Prayer is an earnest hope or wish. It is our prayer that the current progress on human rights will be sustained.

From a Christian or biblical perspective, prayer is our direct point of contact with our God who art in heaven. Prayer is the process that gives us permission to communicate and talk with our God in heaven.

---

1 Merriam Webster
2 Oxford Dictionary

AND WHEN WE PRAY

The methodology of prayer is not a single process where man contacts God without some reciprocation from God. A proper and sincere prayer requires contact between both God and man. Prayer is a mutual action between God and man as defined in Scripture. God sets the parameters and conditions for answered prayer. In formulating prayer, and according to our intent, we must determine what to say and how to say it.

Our reason to pray comes from the instructions and commands God gives through the Scriptures. There are many scriptures that reference prayer and will be mentioned later.

The Purpose of Prayer

There are many reasons why we pray. We often want to talk to God for help to make it through a difficult time, or a depressed feeling, or we pray for some situation that affects our health or wealth. Often, we pray to give thanks to the One who gives life, and to offer an acknowledgement that God is Almighty, Jesus is Lord, and the Holy Spirit leads and guides us into all righteousness.

The more you pray, the more you will learn the power of prayer, the wonder of God in all His magnificence. The more you pray, it brings you to a place of recognizing that it gives you a sense of euphoria to know you have a direct connection to, a direct line to the maker and creator of all things. God the Father is the Blesser of all. Although our individual purposes for praying may vary, the main focus should be to the obedience of God the Father.

What Makes Prayer Effective?

We must be aware of the overall makeup of prayer. What goes into prayer? There first must be an acknowledgement that prayer is a good thing, that it works, and that it causes some sense of comfort or belief that it will accomplish its intended purpose as follows:

Faith/Trust: Having a complete and unwavering sense of confidence in something or someone.

> *"Now faith is the substance of things hoped for, the evidence of things not seen."*
>
> Hebrews 11:1

> *"But without faith it is impossible to please him: for he that cometh to God must believe that he is, and that he is a rewarder of them that diligently seek him."*
>
> Hebrews 11:6

> *"Jesus said unto him, If thou canst believe, all things are possible to him that believeth."*
>
> Mark 9:23

> *"And all things whatsoever ye shall ask in prayer, believing, ye shall receive."*
>
> Matthew 21:22

Adoration/Devotion: Having an attitude of love, reverence, loyalty, and a deep respect for the greatness of God.

> *"After this manner therefore pray ye: Our Father which art in heaven, Hallowed be thy name."*
>
> Matthew 6:9

AND WHEN WE PRAY

"O come, let us worship and bow down: let us kneel before the Lord our maker."

PSALMS 95:6

"Let us therefore come boldly unto the throne of grace, that we may obtain mercy, and find grace to help in time of need."

HEBREWS 4:16

Confession/Contrition: The act or expression of sorrow, being remorseful, admission of guilt for sinful acts we have committed.

"If we confess our sins, he is faithful and just to forgive us our sins, and to cleanse us from all unrighteousness."

1 JOHN 1:9

"And forgive us our debts, as we forgive our debtors."

MATTHEW 6:12

"Have mercy upon me, O God, according to thy lovingkindness: according unto the multitude of thy tender mercies blot out my transgressions. Wash me thoroughly from mine iniquity, and cleanse me from my sin. For I acknowledge my transgressions: and my sin is ever before me. Against thee, thee only, have I sinned, and done this evil in thy sight: that thou mightest be justified when thou speakest, and be clear when thou judgest."

PSALMS 51:1-4

"If I regard iniquity in my heart, the Lord will not hear me."

PSALMS 66:18

The Meaning and Purpose of Prayer

Thanksgiving/Gratefulness: Having gratitude for God's goodness and grace, acknowledging all that He has done for us.

> *"Be careful for nothing; but in every thing by prayer and supplication with thanksgiving let your request be made known unto God."*
>
> Philippians 4:6

> *"Rejoice evermore. Pray without ceasing."*
>
> Thessalonians 5:16-17

> *"Blessed by the God and Father of our Lord Jesus Christ, who hath blessed us with all spiritual blessings in heavenly places in Christ."*
>
> Ephesians 1:3

Supplication/Petition: When our prayers to God are specific as we remain faithful that He hears us and will answer.

> *"Praying always with all prayer and supplication in the Spirit, and watching thereunto with all perseverance and supplication for all saints."*
>
> Ephesians 6:18

> *"And this is the confidence that we have in him, that if we ask any thing according to his will, he heareth us: And if we know that he hear us, whatsoever we ask, we know that we have the petitions that we desired of him."*
>
> 1John 5:14

AND WHEN WE PRAY

"If ye then being evil know how to give good gifts unto your children: how much more shall your heavenly Father give the Holy Spirit to them that ask him?"

Luke 11:13

Intercession/Request: The act of asking for God's help on behalf of others with specific request for those suffering from sickness, persecution, grief. Asking for God's mercy and favor for those in need of comfort and healing.

"I exhort therefore, that first of all, supplications, prayers, intercessions, and giving of thanks, be made for all men. For kings, and for all that are in authority, that we may lead a quiet and peaceable life in all godliness and honesty."

1 Timothy 2:1-2

"But I say unto you, Love your enemies, bless them that curse you, do good to them that hate you, and pray for them which despitefully use you, and persecute you;"

Matthews 5:44

"And seek the peace of the city whither I have caused you to be carried away captives, and pray unto the Lord for it: for in the peace thereof shall ye have peace."

Jeremiah 29:7

Praise/Tribute: A prayer of praise is considered to be the highest form of prayer. Through prayer we give honor and glory to the Most High God for His greatness. Giving tribute to God Almighty without asking or seeking anything.

"I will bless the Lord at all times: his praise shall continually be in my mouth. My soul shall make her boast in the Lord: the humble shall hear thereof, and be glad. O magnify the Lord with me, and let s exalt his name together."
PSALMS 34:1-3

"Bless the Lord, O my soul, and all that is within me, bless his holy name. Bless the Lord, O my soul, and forget not all his benefits: Who forgiveth all thine iniquities; who healeth all thy diseases; Who redeemeth thy life from destruction; who crowneth thee with lovingkindness and tender mercies; Who satisfieth thy mouth with good things; so that thy youth is renewed like the eagle's."
PSALMS 103:3-6

"First, I thank my God through Jesus Christ for you all, that your faith is spoken of throughout the whole world."
ROMANS 1:8

Prayer and The Holy Trinity

The word *Trinity* cannot be found in the Bible but the truth of it can be. While there's only one God, the Trinity consists of three distinct persons, the Father, Son, and Holy Spirit. All are equally omniscient, omnipotent, omnipresent, eternal, and unchanging, but each one has unique functions.

Scripture shows how each member of the Trinity fulfills a specific role and reveals how those three roles interrelate. Let me express this idea in these three terms:

- The Father creates a plan,
- Jesus Christ implements the plan, and
- The Holy Spirit administers the plan.

AND WHEN WE PRAY

While our focus should be on the Father, we cannot disregard the Son and the Spirit. It's perfectly normal to incorporate all three persons of the Trinity when we pray. When we pray, we acknowledge the specific role or function the Trinity plays in our lives.

As shown in Matthew and Luke, Jesus taught his disciple how they should pray, he specifically instructed them to pray to "Our Father in heaven." It was Jesus who told us that our prayers should go directly to God the Father. The Bible teaches although there is only one God, He is manifest in three persons, Father, Son and Holy Spirit. This doctrine known as the Trinity, teaches that each person of the Trinity has different functions in how they interact in the lives of both believers and unbelievers. Although the Bible teaches that prayer should be directed to God the Father, it also teaches that access to the Father can only come through Jesus Christ.

> *"Jesus saith unto him, I am the way, the truth, and the life: no man cometh unto the Father, but by me. If ye had known me, ye should have known my Father also: and from henceforth ye know him, and have seen him.*
>
> JOHN 14:6-7

> *Ye have not chosen me, but I have chosen you, and contained you, that ye should go and bring forth fruit, and that your fruit should remain: that whatsoever ye shall ask of the Father in my name, he may give it to you.*
>
> JOHN 15:16

To put that concept of praying to the Father in perspective, we pray directly to God the Father because that is what Jesus taught us to do. Since Jesus is our high priest and has direct access to God the Father, and because of His sacrifice He now sits at the right hand of God interceding for us. As Christians, we pray to God the Father because He is the provider and source of all things. We end that prayer in the name of Jesus because as our intercessor, He is able to approach God because His blood has covered our sins.

So, while we pray to the Father in Jesus' name, depending on your specific prayer request, we can also acknowledge our reliance on the power of the Holy Spirit to lead, guide and strengthen us in our daily walk.

Jesus is always in the process of pleading our case before the Father the same way a defense attorney would do on our behalf. While Satan the "accuser" is busy accusing and presenting his case against us, Jesus is interceding for us. It is imperative that we remember Jesus is the only mediator between God and man. No one else has the power and authority to intercede before the throne of our Almighty God on our behalf.

Elements That Apply to The Lord's Prayer

According to Dakes Annotated Reference Bible in Matthew 6:9-13 pages 59–60 gives reference to 23[3] easy to understand yet critical components of that prayer:

1. Relationship: Our Father
2. Recognition: which art in heaven
3. Adoration: Hallowed by their name
4. Anticipation: Thy kingdom come
5. Consecration: Thy will be done
6. Universality: in earth

---

[3] Dakes Bible

7. Conformity: as it is in heaven
8. Supplication: Give us
9. Definiteness: this day
10. Necessity: our daily bread
11. Penitence: And forgive us
12. Obligation: our debts
13. Forgiveness: as we forgive
14. Love and mercy: our debtors
15. Guidance: And lead us
16. Protection: not into temptation
17. Salvation: but deliver us
18. Righteousness: from evil
19. Faith: For thine is the kingdom
20. Humility: and the power
21. Reverence: and the glory
22. Timelessness: for ever
23. Affirmation: Amen

Prayer Should Be Specific

Several Bible scriptures are referenced that answer the question of whether prayers should be specific. The following gives clarity to a few of those scriptures:

> *"Now I beseech you brethren, for the Lord Jesus Christ's sake, and for the love of the Spirit, that ye strive together with me in your prayers to God for me.*
>
> *That I may be delivered from them that do not believe in Judaea; and that my service which I have for Jerusalem may be accepted of the saints;*

The Meaning and Purpose of Prayer

That I may come unto you with joy by the will of God, and may with you be refreshed. Now the God of peace be with you all." Amen

Romans 15:30-33

In verse 30, in his visit to Jerusalem and Rome, Paul is asking for three specific things:

- For the Roman Christians to pray for him as he was leaving to go into a hostile environment. This request was a strong one as Paul stresses how critical it was that he receives their cooperation through prayer.
- In verse 31 Paul is adamant about the task ahead, and because he was motivated by doing the work in the Name of Jesus, and out of obedience to God, his request was justified by the right motive. He asked that their prayers include him being welcome and accepted by the saints; and delivered from any harm by those that did not believe in his works. Keep in mind that during this time, there was a division between Jewish Christians and the Gentiles who had recently accepted Christ. He was asking to be received by a unified Spirit of love.
- In verse 32 Paul asked that his journey to Rome might be a safe one. Although He was not afraid of the task ahead of him, he felt a need to ask that he might not encounter any hurt, harm, or danger in his travels. Although Paul knew he might face people who could possibly take his life, he also was aware of that power of intercession through prayer could change whatever conflict he might have to contend with.

AND WHEN WE PRAY

Who Are We Praying To?

Before we can understand the purpose of prayer and why we should pray, we should have some clarity about "whom" it is that we are praying to. It is extremely important that we recognize the importance the Holy Trinity has as we deliver prayer. Prayer can be delivered to all three persons of the Trinity, which are God the Father, God the Son (Jesus Christ Our Lord and Savior) and God the Holy Spirit. To pray an effective prayer, it is extremely important to know ALL THREE persons of the trinity. Why? Because each person of the Trinity has a specific role in our Christian walk.

God the Father, God the Son, and God the Holy Spirit are all established in the Word of God through scripture. For prayer to be effective we should have an understanding of who it is that we expect our prayer to reach, and the reason we are praying to that person.

The proper way for prayer to go forth is to pray to God the Father in the name of Jesus Christ and by the power of the Holy Spirit. Unless you are praying in the Spirit, all prayer should end with asking that prayer in the Name of Jesus. While it is permissible to include the Holy Spirit in your prayer, it is not necessary as the Spirit is the one who helps us with our prayer. Praying in the Spirit enables your prayer to go directly to God by way of Jesus Christ and the Spirit.

> *Likewise the Spirit also helpeth our infirmities: for we know not what we should pray for as we ought: but the Spirit itself maketh intercession for us with groanings which cannot be uttered.*
>
> *And he that searcheth the hearts knoweth what is the mind of the Spirit, because he maketh intercessions for the saints according to the will of God.*
>
> ROMANS 8:26-27

The Meaning and Purpose of Prayer

Even Jesus prayed.

> *At the time Jesus answered and said I thank thee, O Father, Lord of heaven and earth, because thou hast hid these things from the wise and prudent, and has revealed them unto babes. Even so, Father, for so it seemed good in thy sight. All things are delivered unto me of my Father: and no man knoweth the Son, but the Father: neither knoweth any man the Father, save the Son, and he to whomsoever the Son will reveal him.*
>
> MATTHEW 11:25-27

John 14:12-13 are two scriptures sometimes referred to as the Christians "power of attorney" because they hold God's promise of unlimited power through prayer.

> *Verily, I say unto you, He that believeth on me, the works that I do shall he do also; and greater works than these shall he do because I go unto my Father. And whatsoever ye shall ask in my name that will I do that the Father may be glorified in the Son.*
>
> JOHN 14:12-13

> *If you shall ask any thing in my name, I will do it.*
>
> JOHN 14:14

The model prayer of Matthew 6:9 says we should address the Father—After this manner therefore pray ye: Our Father which art in heaven, Hallowed be thy name. The model prayer of Luke. 11:2 says—When ye pray, say, Our Father which art in heaven Hallowed be thy name.

AND WHEN WE PRAY

Who's Will Do We Obey?

In the model prayer of Luke 11:2-4, we pray for His (God's) will to be done in heaven as in earth. We pray He will feed us daily. Not just physical food, but spiritual food, which is His Word. We pray He will forgive us for our sins, but in turn we are instructed to forgive other. There is a lot to unpack in this prayer. Most pray for forgiveness, but few have done the work of forgiving others. It's a compound sentence. One does not come without the other, else we pray in vain. We pray that He strengthen us that we will be led from temptation, that we would be delivered from the evil things of life. And here we see the Holy Trinity at work. While we are asking God the Father, we are asking through the Name of Jesus or God the Son, and we have an expectation that God the Holy Spirit will strengthen us as we go through the temptations of life and fight the wiles of the evil one.

CHAPTER 2

The Importance of Prayer

Does God Hear Our Prayer?
Throughout the scriptures, we know that God the Father is a Supreme Being. He is the Creator of the heavens and the earth. He is the Maker and Creator of all living things. And it is through Christian doctrine that we know it is only through His Son Jesus Christ that we have access to Him, being God the Father. Many mistakenly assume they can render a prayer to "God," and "He" will answer. An ineffective prayer goes nowhere. Many are left to assume that either God did not "hear" them or refused to acknowledge their request. Or some believe that God "chooses" not to answer them and that they are unworthy of receiving an answer. 1 John 5:13-15 contains the key to getting an answer to your prayer.

> *These things have I written unto you that believe on the name of the Son of God; that ye may know that ye have eternal life and that ye may believe on the name of the Son of God. And this is the confidence that we have in him, that if we ask anything according to his will, he heareth us:*

AND WHEN WE PRAY

And if we know that he hear us, whatsoever we ask we know that we have thepetitions that we desired of him.

1 JOHN 5:13-15

Verse 14 gives a clue as to what is expected on our part to get our prayers answered. It implies there is a way in which we can have confidence in God to fulfill His promise. It suggests that we can be assured without a doubt that our prayer will be answered. Now that requires a great deal of the kind of faith or belief needed to expect an answer without wavering. But please notice that we have a compound sentence. The first part gives us the assurance we're looking for; however, the second part gives us the condition upon which we must satisfy. That is "if we ask anything according to his will" we can be assured of an answer. In other words, he only "hears" a prayer that is in line with His will for us.

To know what His will is to know who He is and know what the expectations are for us to fulfill.

Are Christians Required to Pray?

As a matter of practice, prayer usually goes hand in hand with a Godly, Christian walk or lifestyle. God created us with a free will. Although His desire is to have us walk daily in His Word and His will, we are free agents to do as we please. Keep in mind that the things of life can be complex, and God's desire is to help us navigate through this life without having to go through a lifetime of trials and tribulations. Of course, we are destined to have various encounters as we live and breathe, grow, and mature at each stage of life. His Word is designed to keep us from falling into the hands of Satan, who according to the Word is "seeking whom he may devour."

Although many Christian often fail to realize the importance of seeking a "righteous" walk with God; we are free moral agents to live as we choose. But common sense encourages us to recognize that there are consequences to our choices. While we did not have control over our being born into the world, we are, according to scripture, responsible for either our salvation or our damnation.

> *For God so loved the world, that he gave his only begotten Son, that whosoever believeth in him, should not perish, but have everlasting life.*
>
> JOHN 3:16

Some believe that does not apply to them, but it is God's offer to all of mankind, to either accept or reject. Unfortunately, many also fail to accept the reality that as free moral agents, their plight in life is spiritually connected to that acceptance or rejection. It is the will of God that all men who desire to make that choice, be saved. God commands us to repent or perish.

> *"I tell you, Nay: but except ye repent you shall all likewise perish."*
>
> LUKE 13:13

Proverbs 1:29-33 addresses the issue of those who "hate knowledge" and "did not chose the fear of the Lord," those who would turn away from His counsel and despise His instruction. The following verses warns of man's choice to chose God's way or his own way:

> *For they hated knowledge, and did not choose the fear of the Lord. They would none of my counsel: they despised all my reproof. Therefore shall they eat of the fruit of their own way, and be filled with their own devices. For the turning away of*

the simple shall slay them and the prosperity of fools shall destroy them. But whoso hearkeneth unto me shall dwell safely, and shall be quiet from fear of evil.

Proverbs 1:29-33

No man can serve two masters: for either he will hate the one, and love the other; or else he will hold to the one and despise the other. Ye cannot serve God and mammon.

Matthew 6:24

This last scripture makes it clear that we are all engage in spiritual warfare, and by choice we need to decide what we want for our lives. It is up to us to either accept or reject God. For those who reject God, there is no need for pray. For those that accept God, it is then our choice to live according to His will or our own will. Scripture tells us that we would know them by their fruit. That is, those who choose to heed His Word will follow his commands and instructions.

Free Moral Agents

According to the *American Heritage College Dictionary*,[4] to be *free* in terms of "free-moral agency" means to not be controlled by the will of another, independent, not subject to arbitrary interference. From the same dictionary, *moral* is defined as "of or concerned with the judgment of the goodness or badness of human action and character or conforming to standings of what is right or just in behavior." It suggests right principles or conduct. *Agency* means "the means or mode of acting; instrumentality," signifying the state or being of exerting power or, in this case, choice. Taken together, then, a human is an

---

4 American Heritage College Dictionary

instrument of God's creation that is empowered and may voluntarily choose between good and evil. So in accordance with the following scriptures:

> *And if it seem evil unto you to serve the Lord, choose you this day whom ye will serve; whether the gods which your fathers served that were on the other side of the flood, orthe gods of the Amorites, in whose land ye dwell: but as for me and my house, we will serve the Lord.*
>
> JOSHUA 24:15

> *For by grace are ye saved through faith; and that not of yourselves: it is the gift ofGod: Not of works, lest any man should boast. For we are his workmanship, created in Christ Jesus unto good works, which God hath before ordained that we should walk in them.*
>
> EPHESIANS 2:8-10

We have the freedom to choose our destiny the same as we can decide where and what we eat; choose the style of clothing or shoes we wear; pursue our own educational or work profession and the like. God does not keep us confined to be a follower of His word, nor does He demand that we accept His Doctrine. Those who seek after and follow Christianity, do so because God the Holy Spirit pricked our hearts and caused us to seek the walk and righteousness of those things that God has ordained for us.

Everyone is accountable and responsible for the moral or immoral choices they make in life whether they are Christian or not. If one who claims Christianity determines there is no need for forgiveness, and no longer want to follow Jesus, then they risk the loss of the salvation they once knew. This of course raises the question as to whether they were ever truly saved based on the following scriptures:

> *For it is impossible for those who were once enlightened, and have tasted of the heavenly gift, and were partakers of the Holy Ghost, And have tasted the good word of God and the powers of the world to come, If they shall fall away, to renew them again unto repentance; seeing they crucify themselves the Son of God afresh, and put him to an open shame.*
>
> HEBREWS 6:4-6

> *Not every one that saith unto me, Lord, Lord shall enter into the kingdom of heaven; but he that doeth the will of my Father which is in heaven. Many will say to me in that day, Lord, Lord, have we not prophesied in thy name? and in thy name have cast out devils? And in thy name done many wonderful works? And then will I profess unto them, I never knew you: depart from me, ye that work iniquity.*
>
> MATTHEW 7:21-23

> *And they also, if they abide not still in unbelief, shall be grafted in: for God is able to graff them in again.*
>
> ROMANS 11:23

Christians do not have to live in fear of being lost every time they are tempted. Their relationship with God is not in jeopardy of coming to an end every time they fall. But to remain in a right relationship with God, we must acknowledge our sin, confess it, and according to God's word, he is faithful and just to forgive us our sins, and to cleanse us from all unrighteousness. (1 John 1:9)

The Importance of Prayer

There are many reasons why we should pray. One of the most important reasons is because God commands us to pray. If we say we love God, then our desire should be to fellowship with him in prayer, which is our only means of communicating with him. In Colossians 4:2 we are encouraged to *"Continue in prayer, and watch in the same with thanksgiving."* As believers, we know that He is our source. It is through acknowledging him in prayer that we receive His love, comfort, strength, and protection. Our relationship and prayer life with God are a necessary ingredient of our daily walk. In the next verse it tells us to:

> *Watch and pray, that ye enter not into temptation: the spirit indeed is willing, but the flesh is weak."*
>
> MATTHEW 26 6:41, NKJV

Exercising prayer can only strengthen our weakened state. It is through prayer we are able to resist temptation and avoid the enemy's attempt to lure us into sin and disobedience.

We are given a great deal of instructions and commands through scripture that is designed to cause our walk in this life to be a better one. There is no promise that things would be totally problem or worry free, but the intent is to provide a road map that allows for an easier path to getting where we need to go in life.

> *But the God of all grace, who hath called us unto his eternal glory by Christ Jesus, after that ye have suffered a while, make you perfect, stablish, strengthen, settle you.*
>
> 1 PETER 5:10

AND WHEN WE PRAY

This scripture encourages us and expects us to receive the blessings that come from persecution. These experiences cause us to:

1. Walk in perfection
2. Become more established in the faith
3. Gain needed spiritual strength
4. Gain and maintain a good foundation.

1Thessalonians 5:14-23 outline fourteen commands to Christians who believe in the Second Coming of Christ starting with verse 14:

Now we exhort you, brethren, warn them that are unruly, comfort feebleminded, support the weak, be patient toward all men. See that none render evil for evil unto any man; but ever follow that which is good both among yourselves, and to all men. Rejoice evermore. Pray without ceasing. In everything give thanks, for this is the will of God in Christ Jesus concerning you. Quench not the Spirit. Despise not prophesying. Prove all things; hold fast that which is good. Abstain from all appearance of evil.

1 Thessalonians 5:14-23

As Christians, we have a command, a charge to act and/or perform in obedience to the Word of God. The instructions set out in these commands are vital to the believer whether they choose to walk in them or not. Verse 14 is specific in that it instructs us in the following manner:

- It speaks to those who have been unruly and whose disorderly walk has become a hinderance to the church.

- It speaks to those who have become soft hearted, perhaps even fearful, and who are in jeopardy of having their battle(s) overtake them.
- It speaks to those who are in need for Christians who can offer strength in their time of weakness; to offer a perspective to help them when they see they need help. To exercise patience

Verse 15 charges us to refrain from doing evil toward anyone just because they've demonstrated evil against us. But to cling to that which is good as we endeavor to treat all men with respect.

Verse 17 commands us to pray without stopping. That is to always walk in a posture that prayer is ever before us. Now of course we don't pray while sleeping. Nor do we pray while working perhaps at a job where it's not practical for verbal or silent prayer to go forth. However, we can as often as we are able to pray whether verbally out loud or self-consciously when able. And certainly, during designated and/or quiet times that are purposely set aside for prayer. At home, in our room, our prayer closet or wherever we can steal away with Jesus to give reverence to God.

Verse 18 commands us to give thanks for all and in all things. Why? Because this is the will of God for us regarding Christ Jesus.

Verse 19 admonishes us not to hold back the Spirit. One would think it impossible to knowingly hold back the Spirit. But we have the ability to either allow the Spirit to operate or refuse to let it work in us at any given point in time.

In an article by Sam Storms, Pastor from Oklahoma City, Oklahoma, he writes there are at least *Seven Ways to Quench the Spirit*[5]. In this article, he also references Apostle Paul in 1 Thessalonians 5:19-22

---

5 Sam Storms

who states: "Paul says that God has granted to Christians the ability to restrict or release what the Spirit does in the life of the local church. The Spirit comes to us as a fire, either to be fanned into full flame and given the freedom to accomplish his will, or to be doused and extinguished by the water of human fear, control, and flawed theology.

How many of us pause to consider the ways in which we inadvertently quench the Spirit's work in our lives individually and in our churches corporately? Do we church leaders instill fear or courage in the hearts of people by the way we speak and preach and lead? Do we so repeatedly pepper our sermons and small group Bible studies, even our personal conversations, with such dire warnings of charismatic excess that we effectively quench the Spirit's work in their lives? Or, after listening to us and observing how we conduct ourselves in Christian ministry, do they find themselves encouraged, courageous, and confident to step out and take risks they otherwise might not take?

The Spirit obviously desires to work in your life and in your church. To use "Paul's metaphor or analogy, the Spirit is like a fire whose flame we want to be careful not to quench or extinguish. The Holy Spirit wants to intensify the heat of his presence among us, to inflame our hearts and fill us with the warmth of his indwelling power. And Paul's exhortation is a warning to all of us lest we become part of the contemporary bucket brigade that stands ready to douse his activity with the water of legalism, fear, and a flawed theology that, without biblical warrant, claims that his gifts have ceased and been withdrawn"

Pastor Sam Storms cites seven (7) ways we quench the Holy Spirit:

1. We <u>quench the Holy Spirit</u> when we rely decisively on any resource other than the Holy Spirit for anything we do in life and ministry.

2. We <u>quench the Spirit</u> whenever we diminish his personality and speak of him as if he were only an abstract power or source of divine energy.
3. We <u>quench the Spirit</u> whenever we suppress or legislate against his work of imparting spiritual gifts and ministering to the church through them.
4. We <u>quench the Spirit</u> whenever we create an inviolable and sanctimonious structures in our corporate gatherings and worship services, and in our small groups, that does not permit spontaneity or the special leading of the Spirit.
5. We <u>quench the Spirit</u> whenever we despise prophetic utterances (1 Thessalonians 5:20)
6. We <u>quench the Spirit</u> whenever we diminish his activity that alerts and awakens us to glorious and majestic truth that we are truly the children of God (Roman 8:15-16; Galatians 4:4-7).
7. We <u>quench the Spirit</u> whenever we suppress, or legislate against, or instill fear in the hearts of people regarding the legitimate experience of heartfelt emotions and affections in worship.

Verse 20 commands that we "despise not prophesying. This verse admonishes us for having a disregard of the Holy Spirit. Denying its existence, the importance and validity; the value and benefits of prophetic sayings.

When We Should Pray?

Finally my brethren, be strong in the Lord, and in the power of his might. Put on the whole armuor of God, that ye may be able to stand against the wiles of the devil. For we wrestle not against flesh and blood, but against principalities, against powers, against the rulers of the darkness of this world, against spiritual wickedness in high places. Wherefore take unto you the whole armour of God, that ye may be able to withstand in the evil day, and having done all, to stand. Stand therefore, having your loins girt about with truth, and having on the breastplate of righteousness: And your feet shod with the preparation of the gospel of peace: above all, taking the shield of faith, wherewith ye shall be able to quench all the fiery darts of the wicked. And take the helmet of salvation and the sword of the Spirit, which is the word of God:

Ephesians 6:10-17

There is great wisdom, counsel, commands, and instructions addressed in verses 10 through 17. Here, God has not only given instruction, but has commanded that we prepare ourselves for battle. Prepare ourselves for the fight with the enemies that God will show us and promises that we will be able to overcome them. When we are properly armed, we also increase in strength. We are able to stand against all enemies and attacks and have the ability to quench or extinguish every fiery dart of Satan.

Dakes Bible page 375 outlines two Kinds of Armour[6] mentioned in verse Ephesians 10:13:

Defensive Armor for Protection
1. Greek - perifephalaia, the helmet—for the head of various forms embossed with many kinds of figures

---

6 Dakes Bible

2. Greek - zoma, the girdle—for the loins to brace the armor tight against the body, and support daggers, swords, and other weapons
3. Greek - thoraz, the breastplate in two parts—one to cover the breast and the other the back to protect the vital organs of the body. It extended down to the legs.
4. Greek - knemides, brazen boots for the feet to cover the front of the leg. A kind of solea was often used to protect the feet from rocks, thorns, etc.
5. Greek - thureos, shield to protect the body from blows and cuts

Offensive Armor for Conquest:
Greek - machaira, sword or bladed weapon, to destroy the enemy and bring his surrender. Besides the sword, other weapons of offense were used-the spear, lance, battle-ax, club, bow and arrow, and sling.

The Six-fold Christian Armor:
1. Loins girt about with truth (verse 14)
2. Breastplate of righteousness (verse 14)
3. Feet shod with the preparation of the gospel of peace (verse 15)
4. The shield of faith (verse 16)
5. The helmet of salvation (verse 17)
6. The sword of the Spirit, the Word of God (verse 17)

Eric Landstrom's article on Spiritual Warfare and the Celestial City of God[7] gives an excellent comparison and contrast of the truths that each piece of armor symbolizes:

---
7 Eric Lanstrom

AND WHEN WE PRAY

1. **Truth** (verse 14). "Gird your loins with truth."
   The opposite of truth are lies and deception.
2. **Righteousness** (v 14). "Put on the breastplate of righteousness."
   Wickedness and unrighteousness are the opposite of holiness and righteousness.
3. **Peace** (verse 14). Shod your feet with the gospel of peace."
   War and turmoil are the opposite of peace.
4. **Faith** (verse 16). "Taking up the shield of faith."
   Lack of trust and disobedience are the opposite of faith.
5. **Salvation** (verse 17). "Take the helmet of salvation."
   Being lost is the opposite of salvation.
6. **The Word of God** (verse 17). "The sword of the Spirit, which is the Word of God."
7. **A lying spirit:** Taken together, the five contrasts listed above collectively contribute toward diverting and deceiving, a spirit of lies against the Word of God.

If we are to be successful in our fight against the enemy, we must arm ourselves to be effective in battle.

> *Praying always with all prayer and supplication in the Spirit, and watching thereunto with all perseverance and supplication for all saints: And for me, that utterance may be given unto me, that I may open my mouth boldly, to make known the mystery of the gospel. For which I am an ambassador in bonds, that therein I may speak boldly, as I ought to speak.*
>
> EPHESIANS 6:18-20

The Importance of Prayer

We should pray at all times. We should pray without ceasing. We should prepare ourselves before we pray as in Ephesians 6:10-20.

It is imperative that we make time to pray. Find a time and place for prayer like a prayer closet, a den, or a bedroom before bedtime.

Prayer time is whenever and wherever we have declared that we will make time. Whenever we get the unction to pray, we should choose a time and stick to it. While it's important to develop a routine, the best time is whenever the Holy Spirit leads you to pray.

The Benefits of Prayer

Because we need a relationship with God, it is to our benefit, and in our best interest to pray. Our reward for praying comes with knowing we can expect an answer to our pray. Once we build a relationship with God, we can build a record or history of testimonies of having our prayers answered. Our reward comes from the interaction we have with God when He shows us that we can depend on Him keeping his word and promise. His keeping of His word also shows us how much he loves us as we diligently serve him. We should know that no prayer is too big or too small for Him to answer. Luke 1:37 says *"nothing is impossible with God."*

God is never too busy to ignore or dismiss our prayer, as long as it is in His will. There is great reward that comes in knowing how important we are to God.

> *Therefore I say unto you, Take no thought for your life what ye shall eat or what ye shall drink nor yet for your body, what ye shall put on. Is not the life more than meat, and the body more than raiment? Behold the fowls of the air: for they sow not, neither do they reap, nor father into barns, yet your heavenly Father feedeth them. Are ye not much better than they?*
> MATTHEW 6: 25-26

AND WHEN WE PRAY

When we go to God in prayer, we are able to accomplish many things to our benefit. Our worship and praise through prayer gives us a sense of closeness and continued relationship as we communicate with Him. One of my favorite scriptures, 2 Chronicles 7:14 shows us how to get back into relationship with him; how to reconcile ourselves to him.

> *"If my people who are called by my name, will humble themselves and pray and seek My face and turn from their wicked ways, then will I hear from heaven and will forgive their sin and will heal their land."*
>
> 2 C<small>HRONICLES</small> 7:14

It's a scripture that gives great hope to those who have fallen by the wayside, those who have not been diligent about keeping His statutes, those who have backslidden. An opportunity to rededicate and come back into the fold is a great way to become whole again.

Prayer allows us to overcome the forces of evil.

> *"Put on the whole armor of God, that ye may be able to stand against the wiles of the devil. For we wrestle not against flesh and blood, but against principalities, again powers, against the rulers of the darkness of this world, against spiritual wickedness in high places"*
>
> E<small>PHESIANS</small> 6:11-12

James 4:10 tell us to:

> *"Humble yourselves in the sight of the Lord, and he shall lift you up."*

The Importance of Prayer

Keeping ourselves in a place of humility as encouraged in Matthew 18:4

> *"Whosoever therefore shall humble himself as this little child, the same is greatest in the kingdom of heaven."*

The many answered prayers serve as a witness to other who has long doubted the purpose or benefit of prayer. Especially when you have the evidence of tangible instances for others to see. Your pay increase, job promotion, your healed body, new home, new car, debts paid off. When you share those testimonies with others, it becomes a great witness to what God can do in the lives of believers who pray.

CHAPTER 3

Praying in the Spirit

Are We Required To Pray In The Spirit?
According to Scripture, we are commanded to follow after charity, and desire spiritual gifts.
   1 Corinthians 14:4-5
   Galatians 5:16-17:
This I say then, Walk in the Spirit, and ye shall not fulfill the lust of the flesh.

We are encouraged through the scripture to do so. There are many benefits for those who do because praying in the Spirit enables you to speak directly to God. While others do not and will not understand the utterances coming from you, God does. It's a wonderful feeling to know that you are communing with God the Father. Praying in the Spirit is another way of saying, "praying in tongues." It's a great way to strengthen your walk with God and enables you to walk in a life that is Spirit-led.

Praying in The Spirit

Praying in the Spirit is a gift and is not to be exploited by being a "show-off" in church or around others. It's available to every believer and helps you pray God's will to Him.

> *"Likewise the Spirit also helpeth our infirmities: for we know not what we should pray for as we ought but the Spirit itself maketh intercession for us with groanings which cannot be uttered."*
>
> Romans 8:26

Often we pray a selfish prayer as in, God bless mother, father, and our children. God heal my body, God help me get this job, and a multitude of other personal wants and needs, concerns, and issues. When praying in the Spirit, we are led to address other's needs or situations we have no knowledge of, but God knows.

For clarity, praying in the Spirit or praying in tongues is not the same thing as speaking in an "unknown tongues."

> *"But the manifestation of the Spirit is given to every man to profit withal."*
>
> 1 Corinthians 12:7

The gift of tongues in this scripture is given to some for the profit of the corporate body when the speaker speaks to men; while the gift of tongues (as mentioned in 1 Corinthians 14:2) is given to all, and as a devotional prayer language only for the profit of the individual who is having a private conversation with God.

Benefits of Praying in the Spirit

- Praying in the Spirit is a gift from God
- Allows us to make direct contact with God.
- To communicate with God, we must talk in a language He understands.
- Develops the spirit-man and gives you strength to live a Spirit-filled life.
- Empowers us to stand against the works of the devil.

Gifts of the Spirit

According to scripture, there are specific reasons why God gave us Spiritual gifts.

> *Now concerning spiritual gifts, brethren, I would not have you ignorant. Ye know that ye were Gentiles, carried way unto these dumb idols, even as ye were led. Wherefore I give you to understand, that no man speaking by the Spirit of God calleth Jesus accursed: and that no man can say that Jesus is the Lord, but by the Holy Ghost. Now there are diversities of gifts, but the same Spirit. And there are differences of administrations, but the same Lord. And there are diversities of operations, but it is the same God which worketh all in all. But the manifestation of the Spirit is given to every man to profit withal.*
> 1 CORINTHIANS 12:1-7

> *And he gave some, apostles; and some, prophets; and some evangelists; and some, pastors and teachers. For the perfecting*

of the saints, for the work of the ministry, for the edifying of the body of Christ.

EPHESIANS 4:11-15

The Spirit continues to perform as an executive of God to continue the work of Jesus Christ. That work includes seeing that we enjoy the benefits of what God has to offer us when we follow His instructions. 1 Corinthians 12 gives further proof that the Holy Spirit, our Comforter and Helper want to provide us with every opportunity to educate us. We find the function or role of the Spirit is to distribute the "Nine Gifts of the Holy Spirit" and are supernatural gifts according to scripture. They fall into three classifications: The Gifts of Revelations or mind gifts; The Gifts of Inspiration or vocal gifts; and The Gifts of Power or working gifts.

For to one is given by the Spirit the word of wisdom; to another the word of knowledge by the same Spirit; To another faith by the same Spirit; to another the gifts of healing by the same Spirit; To another the working of miracles; to another prophecy; to another discerning of spirits; to another divers kinds of tongues; to another the interpretation of tongues.

1 CORINTHIANS 12:8-10

Gifts of Revelation or "Mind Gifts'

- The Word of Wisdom - A supernatural revelation or insight into God's divine will and purpose, revealing how to solve a problem.
- The Word of Knowledge - A supernatural revelation or insight into God's divine will or plan to know things that could not be known of oneself.

- Discerning of Spirits - The supernatural revelation or insight into the realm of spirits, to detect them and their plan and includes reading the minds of men.

Gifts of Inspiration or "Vocal Gifts"
- Prophecy - The supernatural utterance in the native tongue. It is a miracle of divine utterance, not conceived by human thought or reasoning. It includes speaking unto men to edification, exhortation, and comfort.
- Divers Kinds of Tongues - The supernatural utterance in other languages that are not known to the speaker.
- The Interpretation of Tongues - The supernatural ability to interpret in the native tongue what is uttered in other languages not known by the one who interprets by the Spirit.

Gifts of Power or "Working Gifts"
- The Gift of Faith - The supernatural ability to believe God without human doubt, unbelief, and reasoning.
- The Gift of Healing - The healing of all manner of sickness by supernatural power, without human aid or medicine.
- The Working of Miracles - The supernatural power to intervene in the ordinary course of nature, and to counteract natural laws if necessary.

One major purpose of the Spirit in the New Testament age is to declare and demonstrate the presence of God. This helps to enhance the believer's faith that God is always near and working on our behalf, and it helps the non-believer see that God is near and wanting to be involved in their lives more intimately. These gifts were distributed to man according to how the Spirit determines is best suited for each individual depending on the grace God has placed on them. For example: one who has the gift for being able to show mercy on those who are sick, must be equipped with the ability to show sympathy and cheerfulness.

Other purposes for spiritual gifts within the body of Christ are to build unity within the Church. The intent is for the "body" to be fitly joined together; so that it's imperative each one depends on the other. Where debates, confusion, contention, conflict, or animosity exist, the flesh of man is at work, and further evidence the Spirit is not leading them. Where the Spirit dwells, there is perfect harmony, peace and an atmosphere of love with the Church.

CHAPTER 4

Secrets to Answered Prayer

Secrets to Answered Prayer

FAITH: When we exercise our right to pray, we know that one must also exercise a level of faith, that when they pray, there is an expectation to glean results. Knowing, that faith is something that you cannot see with the visible eye, nor touch in any way. Our ability to "hope" or look forward to results is something we are trusting to happen without fail. Hope coupled with varying level of faith is a belief system that many put into practice. There must be some premise that causes one to believe that by exercising faith, then it's true that will bring forth the expected fruit of their labor or prayer. This truth is based on facts or the Word of God in scripture as being the basis of why we can believe that by "hoping" and putting "faith" into place, we can receive that which we don't have right at this time but can expect later.

> *Now faith is the substance of things hoped for, the evidence of things notseen.*
>
> HEBREWS 11:1

AND WHEN WE PRAY

"faith comes by hearing and hearing by the word of God."
Romans 10:17

But without faith it is impossible to please him: for he that cometh to God must believe that he is, and that he is a rewarder of them that diligently seek him.
Hebrews 11:6

To seek God diligently requires a level of faith that is undeniable, genuine, honest and sincere.

Faith is a must in having a relationship with God. We must first believe that He IS before we can come to him

That the residue of men might seek after the Lord, and all the Gentiles, upon whom my name is called, saith the Lord, who doeth all these things.
Acts 15:17

It's expressed in this verse that God's desire is that a small remnant of Israel, the Gentiles and all Christians would seek after Him and call on His name.

For ye know how that afterward, when he would have inherited the blessing, he was rejected for he found no place of repentance, though he sought it carefully with tears.
Hebrews 12:17

This verse warns us to carefully seek the blessings of God. It's a reflection of the plight of Esau (Genesis 25:24-26) who as the firstborn, was entitled to certain privileges. But Esau showed disdain for what should have been a blessing when he promised to sell his birthright to his younger brother in exchange for a bowl of soup. In the end, he failed to see how his carelessness had consequences, and caused him to lose out on the blessings of God. We cannot continue to walk in a sinful and ungrateful nature without consequences.

> *Of which salvation the prophets have enquired and searched diligently, who prophesied of the grace that should come unto you: Searching what, or what manner of time the Spirit of Christ which was in them did signify, when it testified beforehand the sufferings of Christ, and the glory that should follow.*
> 1PETER 1:10-11

Since there are many whose prayers have gone unanswered, they may be of the mindset that God is illusive, hard to reach, or unwilling to answer. There is no mystery to getting prayers answered; however, there is revelation knowledge that God provides to those who seek it.

> *He answered and said unto them, Because it is given to you to know the mysteries of the kingdom of heaven, but to them it is not given. For whosoever hath, to him, shall be given, and he shall have more abundance: but whosoever hath not, from him shall be taken away even that he hath.*
> MATTHEWS 13: 11-12

There are several reasons why Jesus Christ used parables or stories that one can relate to. These parables and/or stories were effective because they offered illustrations of those comparisons. These comparisons allowed for making truths clear as the hearer is chastised but is able to receive without feeling offended. The tactful way Jesus was able to disseminate these truths included giving historical references along with circumstances that was clearly understood. Because the principles of interpretation was given by Jesus Himself, His words were meant to accomplish the following:

- Revealed truth in a manner that is intended to generate more interest
- Reveals additional new truths to those who have an interest in learning
- Reveals mysteries by giving comparisons to that which is already known
- Conceals the truth from those who are not interested in and/or who rebel against truth.
- Will continue to add truth to those who love and want more of it.
- Take truth away from those who despise and reject truth.
- Was given to fulfill prophecy.

God did not intend for any of us to be ignorant.

> *And his disciples asked him, saying "What might this parable be? And he said, Unto you it is given to know the mysteries of the kingdom of God: but to others in parables; that seeing they might not see, and hearing they might not understand.*
>
> LUKE 8: 9-10

These mysteries[8] according to man can be defined as that which excites curiosity, wonder, etc. but is impossible or difficult to explain or solve, is completely mysterious and altogether incapable of being search out,

---

8 Webster's New World Roget's Thesaurus

interpreted, or understood; but in the ways of God applies to that which is beyond ordinary human understanding or perception in connection with religious rites or spiritual experience.

> *For I long to see you, that I may impart unto you some spiritual gift, to the end ye may be established; That is, that I may be comforted together with you by the mutual faith both of you and me. Now I would not have you ignorant brethren, that oftentimes I purposed to come unto you, (but was let hitherto,) that I might have some fruit among you also, even as among other Gentiles.*
>
> ROMANS 1: 11-13

However, these mysteries according to scripture were not previously known in the Old Testament but are now revealed through the New Testament of Jesus Christ. Below are eighteen of those mysteries of Scripture:

1. The kingdom of heaven and the Kingdom of God (Matthew:13:11, Luke 8:10)
2. Israel's blindness (Romans 11:25)
3. Salvation in Christ (Romans 16:25)
4. The wisdom of God (1 Corinthians 2:7)
5. The doctrines of God (1 Colossians 2:2; 1 Timothy 3:16)
6. The gospel (Ephesians 6:19)
7. Gift of knowledge (1 Corinthians 13:2)
8. Speaking in tongues (1 Corinthians 14:2)
9. The rapture of the church (John 14:1-3, 1 Thessalonians 4:13-16)

10. God's will (Ephesians 1:9)
11. The church (Ephesians 3:1-9)
12. Christ in men (Colossians 2:26-27)
13. Doctrines of Christ (Colossians 4:3)
14. Spirit of lawlessness (2 Thessalonians 2:7)
15. Faith of the gospel (1 Timothy 3:9)
16. Seven candlesticks (Revelations 1:20)
17. God's delay in casting out of Satan (Revelations 10:7; 12:7-17)
18. Mystery of Babylon (Revelation 17:5-7)

Conditions to Answered Prayer

All Christians are encouraged to seek out and "inquire diligently" those truths the prophets were speaking of. While they had salvation, grace, fillings and gifts of the Spirit, they continued to search out and examine even the prophesies they were given for understanding.

- We must please God according to 1 John 5:14-15

And this is the confidence that we have in him, that, if we ask anything according to his will, he heareth us: And if we know that he hear us, whatsoever we ask, we known that we have the petitions that we desire of him.

When we come in confidence, we do not waver, we do not doubt asto what the final outcome will be. We must believe with our wholeheart that He is interested in our welfare and will give all things that are best for us, that are according to His will for us. God will answer each person who demonstrates this level of faith and prays a right prayer. Not just a few, but for all who prays His will. We should base our request on what we know about God's character. We know He's a faithful, great, loving and wonderful God.

- Come to God in the right attitude and with the right motives according to

Let your moderation be known unto all men. The Lord is at hand. Be careful for nothing; but in every thing by prayers and supplication with thanksgiving let your requests be known unto God. And the peace of God which passeth all understanding, shall keep your hearts and minds through Christ Jesus.

PHILIPPIANS 4:5-6

We must come with a display of the Fruit of the Spirit. Demonstrating mildness, patience, kindness, moderation, meekness, and gentleness. We are commanded to let all requests be made known to God—whether it be for material, physical or spiritual needs and wants, everything that concerns us in life for whatever reason. We must confess our sins, so that we come to God with a clean and pure heart.

- Believe that He is according to *John 16:23*

And in that day ye shall ask me nothing. Verily, I say unto you, Whatsoever ye shall ask the Father in my name, he will give it you.

It's okay to remind God of the promises he's made concerning you. He already knows but wants you to communicate in a manner that shows you know what he's capable of. Be bold and pray without doubting as we come to Him with specific requests.

- Believe that He is a rewarder of them that diligently seek Him. If one can believe this as much as he believes in the existence of God, prayer will be granted. If one believes firmly in His existence and doubts His word, he makes Him a liar and God is under no obligation to answer prayer according to James 1:4-8

Fasting and Prayer

The power of "fasting" within the Christian Church is another powerful tool available in the weapons of warfare arsenal. Yet most Christians remain willfully unaware of the significance and power that fasting can be for the believer.

At my church, Living Praise Christian Church, our *2020 30-Day Prayer and Fasting Campaign*[9] presents details along with specific instructions and purpose for fasting.

- **Understanding Fasting: Fasting Is One of the Pillars of the Christian Faith**

    It is mentioned in Scripture one-third as much as prayer. Yet most believers put fasting in the background of their lives. Fasting used to be seen as valuable and significant in the Christian church. Now it has become a lost art. So little is taught and practiced in regard to fasting that it is not understood by most believers especially young Christians who are just

---
9 Linda G. Hodge

coming into the body of Christ. They don't hear about or see any older believers fasting, so they conclude that it is something that has only historic significance.

Fasting should be a natural part of the life of a believer. In the same way that we practice the habits of reading the Bible and prayer, we should also practice the habit of fasting. Fasting is intentional abstinence from eating. Sometimes people confuse hunger with fasting. They will say, "Well, I was so busy that I didn't eat today. I'll make that a fast." That wasn't a fast, because you had planned to eat but just didn't have the time. In the Old Testament, the Hebrew word for fast is it sum. It means, "to cover over the mouth." A fast is a conscious, intentional decision to abstain for a time from the pleasure of eating in order to gain vital spiritual benefits. True fasting involves the following:

- **Seeking God**
  First, fasting is a time set apart to seek the face of God. It means abstaining from other things that you find pleasure in for the purpose of giving your whole heart to God in prayer. When you fast, you're telling God, "My prayer and the answers I'm seeking are more important than my pleasure in eating."

  Put God First
  Second, fasting means putting God first, focusing all your attention on Him alone not on His gifts or blessings, but on God Himself. It shows God how much you love and appreciate Him. In this way, fasting is a point of intimacy with God. God will reveal Himself only to people who want to know Him. He says, "You will seek me and find me when you seek me with all your heart." (Jeremiah 29:13)

- **Creating An Environment For Prayer**
  Third, fasting is a time to foster a sensitive environment for the working of prayers. Whenever you read about fasting in the Bible, it always has the word prayer coupled with it.

- **The Result of Fasting**
  Fasting enables us to increase our spiritual capacity. It exerts discipline over our physical appetite. It brings the body under subjection to what the Spirit desires. We are spirits but we live in bodies. Most of the time our bodies control us. When you fast, your spirit increases its control over your body. Fasting enables you to discipline your body so that the body becomes a servant of the Lord, rather than the master of your spirit. Your body begins to obey your spirit rather than its own impulses and habits.

Instructions to add fasting to prayer derives from the conversation Jesus has with His disciples as outlined in Matthews 17:14-21.

And when they were come to the multitude, there came to him a certain man, kneeling down to him, and saying, Lord, have mercy on my son, for he is lunatick, and sore vexed: for ofttimes he falleth into the fire, and oft into the water, And I brought him to thy disciples, and they could not cure him. Then Jesus answered and said, O faithless and perverse generation, how long shall I be with you? How long shall I suffer you? Bring him hither to me. And Jesus rebuked the devil; and he departed out of him; and the child was cured from that very hour. Then came the disciples to Jesus apart, and said, Why could not we cast him out? And Jesus said unto them, Because of your unbelief: for verily I say unto you, if ye have faith as a grain of mustard seed, ye shall say unto this mountain, Remove hence to yonder place; and it shall remove; and nothing shall be impossible unto you. Howbeit this kind goeth not out but by prayer and fasting.

According to *Dake's Bible*[10], fasting is a biblical doctrine that humbles the soul before God. Psalms 69:10 says fasting and prayer is the cure for unbelief. In addition, fasting accomplishes the following:

- It chastens the soul and crucifies the appetite and denies them so as to give the entire time to prayer (Psalms 69:10)
- It manifests earnestness before God to the exclusion of all else (1 Corinthian 7:5)
- Shows obedience and gives the digestive system a rest (Matthew 6:16-18)
- It demonstrates the mastery of man over appetites, aids in victory over temptation, helps to attain power over demons, develops faith, crucifies unbelief and aids in prayer (Matthew 4:1-11; 17)

While all believers should fast, there has not been any rule or regulation given as to how long or how often. Fasting should be determined by individual desire and needs, (i.e.) when in danger, when worried, in trouble, or while in spiritual conflict.

Since fasting and prayer are so prominent in the Bible, modern Christians should do more of this until they receive power with God over all the powers of the devil. Many things about fasting and its

---

10 Dakes Bible

benefits are not known to modern men, but those through the ages who have been men of great prayer also fasted much."

The Bible lists as many as thirty-five times various persons and/or groups fasted and prayed to accomplish their desire.

Why Are Some Prayers Not Answered?

Because prayers are such an important part in the lives of Christians, it's amazing that so many have a lack of understanding as to why their prayers have not been answered. The following are just a few of the many reasons why some prayers go unanswered, and possible scriptural solutions to correct the situation:

- **When a prayer is not in God's will.**

    But seek ye first the kingdom of God, and his righteousness; and all these things shall be added unto you.

    MATTHEW 6:33

    And this is the confidence that we have in him, that, if we ask anything according to his will, he heareth us: And if we know that he hear us, whatsoever we ask, we know that we have the petitions that we desired of him.

    1 JOHN 5:14-15

- **When we walk in pride and refuse to walk in humbleness.**

    A man's pride shall bring him low, but honour shall uphold the humble in spirit.

    PROVERBS 29:23

Humble yourselves in the sight of the Lord, and he shall lift you up.

JAMES 4:10

If my people which are called by my name, shall humble themselves, and pray, and seek my face, and turn from their wicked ways; then will I hear from heaven, and will forgive their sin, and will heal their land.

2 CHRONICLES 7:14

- **When we pray with wrong motives or make ungodly requests.**

  Ye ask, and receive not, because ye ask amiss, that ye may consume it upon your lusts.

  JAMES 4:3

Every way of a man is right in his own eyes: but the Lord pondereth the hearts.

PROVERBS 21:2

- **Remain rebellious while continuing to walk in sin:**

  For the eyes of the Lord are over the righteous, and his ears are open unto their prayers: but the face of the Lord is against them that do evil.

  1 PETER 3:12

The way of the wicked is an abomination unto the Lord: but he loveth him that followeth after righteousness.

PROVERBS 15:9

AND WHEN WE PRAY

But the wicked are like the troubled sea, when it cannot rest, whose waters cast up mire and dirt.
Isaiah 57:20

- **Walking in doubt and refuse to believe the Word of God.**
For verily I say unto you. That whosoever shall say unto this mountain, Be thou removed, and be thou cast into the sea, and shall not doubt in his heart, but shall believe that those things which he saith shall come to pass: he shall have whatsoever he saith. Therefore I say unto you, What things soever ye desire, when ye pray, believe that ye receive them, and ye shall have them.
Mark 11:23-24

- **Refuse to hear the truth of God's Word.**
Because I have called, and ye refused; I have stretched out my hand, and no man regarded; But ye have set at nought all my counsel, and would none of my reproof:
Proverbs 1:24-25

Therefore shall they eat of the fruit of their own way, and be filled with their own devices.
Proverbs 1:31

He that turneth away his ear from hearing the law, even his prayer shall be abomination.
Proverbs 28:9

Secrets to Answered Prayer

- **Refusing to forgive others.**
  And when ye stand praying, forgive if ye have ought against any: that your Father also which is in heaven may forgive you your trespasses. But if ye do not forgive, neither will your Father which is in heaven forgive your trespasses.
  MARK 11:25-26

  Then came Peter to him, and said, Lord, how oft shall my brother sin against me, and I forgive him? till seven times? Jesus saith unto him, I said not unto thee, Until seven times: but, Until seventy times seven.
  MATTHEW 18:21-22

- **Having a lack of faith.**
  Verily, verily, I say unto you, He that believeth on me, the works that I do shall he do also; and greater works than these shall he do: because I go unto my Father. And whatsoever ye shall ask in my name, that will I do, that the Father may be glorified in the Son. If ye shall ask anything in my name, I will do it.
  JOHN 14:12-14

  But without faith it's impossible to please him, for he that cometh to God must believe that he is, and that he is a rewarder of them that diligently seek him.
  HEBREW 11:6

- **Pray a hypocritical prayer to show off or get attention.**
  And when thou prayest, thou shalt not be as the hypocrites: for they love to pray standing in the synagogues and in the

corners of the streets, that they may be seen of men. But thou, when thou prayest, enter into thy closet, and when thou hast shut thy door, pray to the Father which is in secret, and thy Father which seeth in secret shall reward thee openly.

MATTHEW 6:5-6

- **Going to God in prayer with unconfessed sin in one's life.**
  But your iniquities have separated between you and your God, and your sins have hid his face from you, that he will not hear.

ISAIAH 59:2

If I regard iniquity in my heart, the Lord will not hear me:

PSALM 66:18

There can be many reasons why prayers are not answered. Those mentioned above are just a few that do not include tempting or provoking God, forsaking God, marital strife, being vain, failing to pay tithes and many others. One of the best ways to know if our prayers are getting through to God, is to read and practice 2 Corinthians 13:5-6

Examine yourselves, whether ye be in the faith; prove your own selves. Know ye not your own selves, how that Jesus Christ is in you, except ye be reprobates? But I trust that ye shall know that we are not reprobates.

If you say you have accepted Jesus Christ as your personal Savior, then he is in you and you are a new creature. Your daily walk, your works, and your conversation will prove you out.

Does God Have Limits?

The short answer to that question is no, except where He has limited himself. Those limits concern only those areas where He will not and cannot go back on His Word. Since we were created to be free agents, we are free to either accept or reject what God has offered all mankind.

God knows all, sees all, and is able to do all things, there is technically nothing that restricts God. However, God will not go against His own laws and principles. Because God has set in place specific perfections that benefit us, and are in our best interest, God cannot and will not go back on His own Word. His character makes it impossible to operate outside the order He himself has ordained for us to walk. The wisdom of God will always cause Him to order our steps in accordance with His will for us. And, because of His holiness, He will not, and cannot lie or break the laws He Himself has set for us to abide by. According to scripture, the following represent just a few of those limitations God has placed on himself:

He Cannot:

1. Pledge that every saved man will continue in Christ (John 1:18; Galatians 1:6-8)
2. Eliminate any reaping for what is sown (Romans 8:12-13; Galatians 6:7-8)
3. Lie (Hebrews 6:17-19)
4. Be unrighteous (Romans 9:14)
5. Change His own eternal plan (Acts 15:18; Ephesians 2:7)
6. Forgive unconfessed sin (Luke 13:1-5)
7. Consent to hypocrisy ((Isaiah 1:13)
8. Cast down a repentant soul that comes in faith (John 6:37)

AND WHEN WE PRAY

9. Demand anyone to serve God against their own will (1 Timothy 2:4; John 3:16)
10. Cancel out free moral agency and moral responsibility (1 John 1:7; Romans 6:16-23)
11. Save those who walk in rebellion or who reject God's doctrine (Matthew 18:3)
12. Judge the righteous along with the wicked (Genesis 19:22; Revelations 20:5-6)
13. Keep one saved from sin if they choose to go back into sin (Romans 6:16-23; Hebrews 6:4-9)
14. Have respect of persons (James 2:9-10)
15. Deny Himself (2 Timothy 2:13)
16. Be tempted with evil (James 1:13-15)

CHAPTER 5

Tools to Use in Battle

Lessons on Prayer

There are three essential parts to an effectual fervent prayer: ask, seek, and knock.

1. **ASK:** You need to ask the will of God: The only way to ask His will is to know His will. Knowing His will and refusing to walk in His will is deliberate and can cause your prayer to be hindered.
   James 4:17—Therefore to him that knoweth to do good, and doeth it not, to him it is sin.
2. **SEEK:** Diligently seek God's answer
3. **KNOCK:** Put that answer into action.

Those key requirements are given in Matthew 7:7-11.

Ask, and it shall be given you, seek, and ye shall find; knock, and it shall be opened unto you: For every one that asketh receiveth; and he that seeketh findeth; and to him that knocketh it shall be opened.

AND WHEN WE PRAY

It is God's will that we ask and get what we want. We should put our whole heart into seeking, asking with trust and belief without doubt, with an attitude of humbleness.

Other lessons to learn include the many scriptures that encourage us to stay within the confines of the principles of prayer. By doing so we can be sure of the following:

- Have confidence in knowing as long as we do not waver or have doubt that God will deliver what we've asked for, our prayers will be answered.
- Have confidence that God the Father is concerned with His children and their welfare. That means He is prepared to give us His best when we ask according to His will for us.
- When we are relentless about pursuing the promises of God.

Most Effective Bible Verses For Prayers

Two of the most memorable Bible verses on prayer and often referred to as "The Lord's Prayer" is contained in the Books of Matthew and Luke.

Matthew 6:9-13: Considered to be the "model" prayer

After this manner therefore pray ye: Our Father which art in heaven, Hallowed be they name. Thy kingdom come. Thy will be done in earth as it is in heaven. Give us this day our daily bread. And forgive us our debts as we forgive our debtors. And lead us not into temptation, but deliver us from evil: For thine is the kingdom, and the power, and the glory, forever. Amen.

Luke 11:2-4—these scriptures follow verse 1 where one of the disciples of Jesus said unto him, "Lord, teach us to pray."

Tools to Use in Battle

And he said unto them When ye pray, say, Our Father which art in heaven, Hallowed be they name. Thy kingdom come. Thy will be done, as in heaven, so in earth. Give us day by day our daily bread. And forgive us our sins for we also forgive every one that is indebted to us. And lead us not into temptation but deliver us from evil.

The following scriptures are excellent material that covers most of our desires to include in prayers for redemption, for healing, for encouragement, to strengthen our daily walk, for protection when we feel the weight of persecution, and much more. These scriptures are important because they not only show the want or need prayed for, but also in most cases, show the results of that prayer. The uses of these scriptures become personal and powerful prayers because we can see ourselves in each one.

If my people, which are called by my name, shall humble themselves, and pray, and seek my face, and turn from their wicked ways; then will I hear from heaven, and will forgive their sin, and will heal their land.

2 Chronicles. 7:14

Praying always with all prayer and supplication in the Spirit, and watching thereunto with all perseverance and supplication for all saints: And for me, that utterance may be given unto me, that I may open my mouth boldly, to make known the mystery of the gospel.

Ephesians 6:18-19

AND WHEN WE PRAY

Then shall ye call upon me and ye shall go and pray unto me, and I will hearken unto you. And ye shall seek me, and find me when you shall search for me with all your heart.

JEREMIAH 29:12-13

Confess your faults one to another, and pray one for another, that ye may be healed. The effectual fervent prayer of a righteousness man availeth much.

JAMES 5:16

If I regard iniquity in my heart, the Lord will not hear me.

PSALM 66:18

Therefore I say unto you, What things soever ye desire, when ye pray believe that ye receive them and ye shall have them.

MARK 11:24

The eyes of the Lord are upon the righteous and his ears are open unto their cry.

PSALM 34:15

The sacrifice of the wicked is an abomination to the Lord, but the prayers of the upright is his delight.

PROVERBS 15:8

And straightway the father of the child cried out and said with tears, Lord, I believe; help thou mine unbelief.

MARK 9:24

Tools to Use in Battle

He will regard the prayer of the destitute, and not despise their prayer.

PSALM 102:17

Rejoicing in hope; patient in tribulation; continuing instant in prayer;

ROMANS 12:12

O my God, incline thine ear, and hear: open thine eyes and behold our desolations, and the city which is called by they name: for we do not present our supplications before thee for our righteousness, but for thy great mercies.

DANIEL 9:18

And this is the confidence that we have in him, that, if we ask anything according to his will, he heareth us. And if we know that he hear us, whatsoever we ask, we know that we have the petitions that we desired of him.

1 JOHN 5:14-15

The Lord is nigh unto all them that call upon him to all that call upon him in truth.

PSALM 145:18

Give ear to my words O Lord, consider my meditation. Hearken unto the voice of my cry, my King, and my God: for unto thee will I pray. My voice shalt thou hear in the morning, O Lord; in the morning will I direct my prayer unto thee and will look up.

PSALM 5:3

Ye ask and receive not, because ye ask amiss, that ye may consume it upon your lusts.

JAMES 4:3

Weapons of Warfare

Apostle Paul gives insight into how we can use divine power as weapons of warfare when we exert the authority given by God through Christ Jesus. In 2 Corinthians 10:1-6 of The Holy Bible, New Living Translation, and Paul gives clarity as he defends his authority.

Now I, Paul, appeal to you with the gentleness and kindness of Christ though I realize you think I am timid in person and bold only when I write from far away. Well, I am begging you now so that when I come I won't have to be bold withthose who think we act from human motives. We are human, but we don't wagewar as humans do. We use God's mighty weapons, not worldly weapons, toknock down the strongholds of human reasoning and to destroy false arguments. We destroy every proud obstacle that keeps people from knowing God. Wecapture their rebellious thoughts and teach them to obey Christ.And after youhave become fully obedient, we will punish everyone who remainsdisobedient.

In Verse 4, Dakes Bible outlines four great Conquest of Spiritual Weapons[11]

1. **Destruction of strongholds** - We destroy reasonings of pagan philosophers and Jewish rabbis and their

---

11 Dakes, page 346

dogmas that nullify the word of God and the facts of the Gospel. These fortifications we pull down and demolish. We put to flight the demon powers and alien armies, raising the banner of the cross high on the field of battle. (verse 4)

2. **Casting down imaginations** - We demolish all theories, reasonings, and any high system of ethics, religion, mythology, metaphysics, sublime doctrines, or philosophy set forth to defy the knowledge of God (verse 5).

3. **Bringing into captivity** every thought to the obedience of Christ - We take every thought prisoner and lead it into captivity to obey Christ (verse 5). Lascivious, vain and evil thoughts of all kinds are brought down and made obedient to His laws. That includes any thinking that is contrary to virtue, purity and righteousness.

4. **Having in readiness to avenge all disobedience** - We stand at all times ready, so to speak, to court-martial any opposing the Gospel of Christ, after separating ourselves from them (verse 6). The picture here is that of a strong fortified city where the enemy makes his last stand; entrenching himself about the walls; raising towers and preparing engines of defense and offense upon the walls to insure victory. The fortifications, walls, towers, and castles are taken by the Gospel and the whole opposition is destroyed and taken captive.

AND WHEN WE PRAY

Knowing how to get our prayers answered is actually not a secret at all. God provides us with the right combination through the Scripture. There are conditions to having our prayers answered.

Ephesians 6:10-20 lays out God's plan for us to arm ourselves when on the "battlefield" of life. There are specific pieces of armour to use in our battles, as well as to guard ourselves with throughout the various fights we will encounter. If we look at the "armour" from a military perspective, each piece has a distinct purpose in protecting us while in battle.

> *Finally, my brethren, be strong in the Lord, and in the power of his might. Put on the whole armour of God, that ye may be able to stand against the wiles of the devil.*
>
> EPHESIANS 6:10-11

It is here the word tells us who our enemies are so that we are not left in the dark. Here we are given specific instructions on how to combat and defeat the tricks and schemes of the devil.

God is showing us how to stand up against all of our enemies whenever and wherever we may be attacked.

> *For we wrestle not against flesh and blood, but against principalities, against powers, against the rulers of the darkness of this world, against spiritual wickedness in high places. Wherefore, take unto you the whole armour of God, that ye may be able to withstand in the evil day, and having done all to stand. Stand therefore, having your loins girt about with truth, and having on the breastplate of righteousness;*
>
> EPHESIANS 6: 12-14

Tools to Use in Battle

We support our bodies with daily doses of truth: teaching truth, preaching truth, walking in truth at all times. The breastplate covers both the front and back of our bodies to protect the vital organ including the heart to insure nothing gets in to harm us.

Verse 15 – *And your feet shod with the preparation of the gospel of peace;*

Having our feet shod in the preparation of the gospel of peace guarantees a faithful Christian walk. We have to stay fully prepared at all times as we anticipate the Second Coming of Christ.

Verse 16 – *Above all taking the shield of faith, wherewith ye shall be able to quench all the fiery darts of the wicked.*

The shield of faith is meant to protect us from the fiery darts of the persecutions we face often on a daily basis. The reference to "darts" is equivalent to a spear, a weapon or any sharp instrument thrown at us. These include different temptations that cross our path to get us off course. The "shield" is a defensive or offensive mechanism to protect us against the tricks of the wicked.

Verse 17 – *And take the helmet of salvation, and the sword of the Spirit, which is the word of God.*

The helmet is meant to guard your mind from unclean or evil thoughts that attempt to seep in from time to time. Stay prepared by using the "word" every day to rebuke, defend, admonish and strengthen against attacks. The written word of God has always been, and always will be our greatest defense again the enemy.

Verse 18 – *Praying always with all prayer and supplication in the Spirit, and watching thereunto with all perseverance and supplication for all saints.*

Although prayer is not considered to be part of the actual "armour," it is still a necessary tool to be used in the fights we encounter on the battlefield. We must not only establish an effective prayer life, but also be consistent and dedicated to carrying out that mandate. Stay strong and persevere until your prayer is answered. Prayer for the believer is a critical tool as a weapon of warfare.

> *And for me, that utterance may be given unto me, that I may open my mouth boldly, to make known the mystery of the gospel. For which I am an ambassador in bonds that therein I may speak boldly, as I ought to speak.*
>
> EPHESIANS 6:19-20

> *And hereby we know that we are of the truth, and shall assure our hearts before him.*
>
> *For if our heart condemn us, God is greater than our heart and knoweth all things. Beloved, if our heart condemn us not then have we confidence toward God. And whatsoever we ask we receive of him, because we keep his commandments, and do those things that are pleasing in his sight.*
>
> 1 JOHN 3:19-22

> *Let your moderation be known unto all men. The Lord is at hand. Be careful for nothing: but in every thing by prayer and supplication with thanksgiving let your requests be made known unto God.*
>
> PHILIPPIANS 4:5-6

Verse 5 is a reminder and an admonishment that God sees all and knows all. We should all govern ourselves accordingly. Verse 6 tell us not to stress or worry, because God is there to help us through anything.

But let patience have her perfect work, that ye may be perfect and entire, wanting nothing. If any of you lack wisdom, let him ask of God that giveth to all men liberally and upbraideth not: and it shall be given him. But let him ask in faith nothing wavering, For he that wavereth is like a wave of the sea driven with the wind and tossed. For let not that man think that he shall receive any thing of the Lord. A double-minded man is unstable in all his ways.

JAMES 1:4-8

The scriptures in James above also outlines what it takes to get your prayers answered. We must believe without doubting, that God is a rewarder to those who diligently trust in Him. Verses 4 through 8 illuminates seven ways to get an answer to prayers:

1. Pray to the Father
2. Ask in the name of Jesus
3. Pray and ask by the Holy Spirit
4. Pray with full understanding of the rights and privileges available
5. Pray in harmony with the Word of God
6. Pray in faith and without doubt
7. Pray with praise for the answer even before it comes.

Fruit of the Spirit

As Comforter and Helper, the Spirit wants to ensure we have all the tools that will keep us in harmony with God's Word and God's will. One of the many goals and functions of the Spirit is to provide us with the strength needed to accomplish a fruitful and successful walk with Jesus Christ and gaining the approval from God the Father.

AND WHEN WE PRAY

Fruit in this context are not edible fruits or vegetables but shows the result or action from our deeds or hard work. The "fruit of our labor" implies we have something to show for our work other than a paycheck.

Paul lists the nine specific behaviors that should result from our work as Christians.

1. **Love:** According to Greek interpretations, this love is not a brotherly (philos) love, or sexual (eros) love, but a perfect (agape) love that only God can give. Agape love harnesses a desire to help others. Biblical love is a choice that expresses itself in loving ways, and always seeks the welfare of others.

Fulfil ye my joy, that ye be likeminded, having the same love, being of one accord, of one mind.
PHILIPPIANS 2:2

2. **Joy:** This type of joy celebrates God's favor and grace and expresses the happiness that is not the result of anything that we've done for ourselves.

My brethren, count it all joy when ye fall into divers temptations; Knowing this, that the trying of your faith worketh patience.
JAMES 1:2-3

3. **Peace:** With God, the Spirit of peace is possible no matter what our circumstances may be. With God, we are able to experience peace, safety and security. With God's peace we don't fear the instability the circumstances that life often brings.

Tools to Use in Battle

For to be carnally minded is death; but to be spiritually minded is life and peace.

ROMANS 8:6

4. **Longsuffering:** The Spirit empowers us to endure the challenges, provocations, offenses and injuries we encounter on a daily basis without resentment or murmuring. We are able to demonstrate our ability to persevere.

Howbeit for this cause I obtained mercy, that in me first Jesus Christ might shew forth all longsuffering, for a pattern to them which should hereafter believe on him to life everlasting.

1 TIMOTHY 1:16

5. **Gentleness:** One who has a disposition of being soft-spoken, not boisterous, even-tempered, and presents themselves as being gracious in mannerisms.

In meekness instructing those that oppose themselves, if God peradventure will give them repentance to the acknowledging of the truth.

2 TIMOTHY 2:25

6. **Kindness:** This characteristic also implies gentleness or someone who behaves properly, has moral integrity without getting caught in self-righteousness or judgment. One who is virtuous and generous, and God-like in life and conduct.

AND WHEN WE PRAY

That in the ages to come he might shew the exceeding riches of his grace in his kindness toward us through Christ Jesus.
EPHESIANS 2:7

7. **Faith:** A character trait that combines dependability and trust based on our confidence in God and His eternal faithfulness. It is our belief in God and our certainty that Jesus is the Messiah whom we obtain eternal salvation.

Wherefore also we pray always for you, that our God would count you worthy of this calling, and fulfil all the good pleasure of his goodness, and the work of faith with power.
2 THESSALONIANS 1:1

8. **Meekness:** Characterizes one who has been placed in a position of weakness, but able to show strength by maintaining control.

Brethren, if a man be overtaken in a fault, ye which are spiritual, restore such a one in the spirit of meekness; considering thyself, lest thou also be tempted.
GALATIANS 6:1

9. **Temperance:** One who is able to exercise self-control of the flesh. To say no to flesh gives us the power to say yes to the Spirit.

Tools to Use in Battle

This I say then, Walk in the Spirit, and ye shall not fulfil the lust of the flesh.

GALATIANS 5:16

God and Jesus Christ sent the Spirit to lead and empower all Christians. The fruit of the Spirit is produced by the Spirit to enable us to manifest all of the characteristics of Christ as we grow. The Spirit knows we need time to grow and mature as edible fruit does but is there to strengthen us as we fight against the obstacles we encounter from day to day. As we submit ourselves to the Spirit, His goal remains to shape and mold us into the image of Christ.

CHAPTER 6

Prayer is Personal

There's Personality In Prayer

We should all take a personal interest in prayer because it is the Word and the Will of God that says so. All of our voices are unique to God, He knows us by name when we pray to Him. Each of us has a signature approach, a personality designed by God that gets His attention when we come to the throne of grace. The Word of God says:

> *And fear not them which kill the body, but are not able to kill the soul; but rather fear him which is able to destroy both soul and body in hell, Are not two sparrows sold for a farthing? And one of them shall not fall on the ground without your Father. But the very hair of your head are all numbered. Fear ye not therefore, ye are of more value than many sparrows. Whosoever therefore shall confess me before men, him will I confess also before my Father which is in heaven.*
>
> MATTHEW 10:28-32

God's love for us is so great, and because He values us more than anything on earth, and promises to watch over us at all times. Since God values something as trivial as a sparrow, then how awesome is His love for us. To know the number of hairs on our heads, one would have to pay extraordinary attention. This gives more proof of God's wisdom and love for us and continues to monitor the smallest detail when it concerns each of us.

It's a small sacrifice on our part to return God's love by following His commands for us. His commands are in our best interest to live our life protected by the Almighty hand of God. To fully understand God, you need to know the Heart of God. Understanding this will allow you to see a little deeper into the things of God and how His plan is intended to work in your favor. As the Creator of man, God has our welfare before Him at all times because he wants what is best for us. His plan comes from His heart and will get us to where we need to be in life. To oppose His plan, will only delay the blessings He has in store for us.

God makes Himself known through the Scriptures, and reveals what we can expect from Him, as well as what He expects from us. Genesis 3:9 is a great example of His loving care as a Father. After Adam and Eve had disobeyed God and hid themselves, God asked, "where are you?"

One of the characteristics of a father is to reach out to his children. He wants to know what we're doing, to verify that all in well with us. Because God is concerned about our relationship with Him, He will come looking for us. God the Son also has a passion to stay in a relationship with us. Even if we are the one who has broken the relationship with Him. Like His Father, Jesus has a heart that seeks to keep us close.

Prayer is Personal

The question "where are you?" as an individual, caused me to reflect on myself as well as others. The thought came to me, how can I be sure that God knows me, how can I be sure that He remembers me? How can I be sure that God is taking a personal interest in me?

So, that when you go to Him in prayer, it's an honest, earnest prayer or petition because you know who He is, and what He's capable of performing on your behalf. I've concluded we all need to give God a reason to remember us by name as He remembered Noah. There are several people God Remembers in the Bible, but to mention a few:

Genesis 8:1: **God remembered Noah** and caused the flood to cease.

Genesis 30:22: **God remembered Rachel** when He saw she was in turmoil because of being barren and not able to bear a child. God opened her womb, and she was able to conceive.

1 Samuel 1:8: **God remembered Hannah.** Hannah had reason to cry out to God for an answer as to why her womb had been closed. She knew that the path to motherhood also equated to her womanhood and being without child she felt less than. But her prayers did not fall on deaf ears when she vowed to God, and through her prayer and supplication, would dedicate her child back to Him. God answered Hannah when she became pregnant with Samuel.

Genesis 18:23 and 19:29: **God remembered Abraham** who prayed and asked God if He would destroy the righteous along with the wicked concerning Sodom and Gomorrah. In this intercessory prayer, Abraham's encounter with God results in both positive and negative answers. God revealed to Abraham that He would destroy them because of the wickedness of those cities. Many believe that God wanted to destroy those cities due to the practice of homosexual sins and other immoralities only. But they were judged based on several transgressions against God. Some of those iniquities compared to the sinfulness of Israel, are referenced in Ezekiel 16:49-50:

1. Corruption
2. Prideful
3. Fulness of bread and abundance of idleness
4. Without pity for the poor and needy
5. Arrogance
6. Committed many abominations
7. More wicked than Samaria

Abraham had great compassion for the people of Sodom and Gomorrah to include his own family. He went boldly to God as he tried to bargain with God to spare them if he could first find fifty righteous people. He pressed further, that if he could find forty-five, then forty, thirty, twenty and eventually ten righteous people. This prayer shows that we can influence God to change his. Keeping in mind of course, that God will never do anything that goes against his own character. In addition to Abraham and his family, God spared his nephew, Lot, and his wife on Abraham's behalf. Although it was God's intention to spare Lot's wife, she died when she disobeyed God's instruction to not look back on the city as it was being destroyed. She did and was turned into a pillar of salt.

To have the favor of God, we must adhere to His Word and commands. There are many commands given by God, some of the most significant are as follows:

- Repent and believe - Matthew 4:17
- Follow me - Matthew 4:19
- Love your enemies - Matthew 5:12

- Pray for those who persecute you - Matthew 5:44
- Be baptized - Matthew 28:19
- Pray - Matthew 6:9-13
- Go ye therefore - Matthew 28:19-20
- Love - Matthew 22:37-39
- Take of the Lord's Supper - Luke 22:19-20
- Give cheerfully - Luke 6:38

These God-given commands and are not optional, but are equivalent to instructions, directions, orders, mandates, and missions, to be carried out accordingly. If we want God to notice us, to hear our prayers and petitions, it's only right that we should exercise a voice that He has become accustomed to.

What Can Prayer Accomplish?
The following represent several examples of those who petitioned God in prayer and received an answer.

Hannah (I Samuel 1:8-18)
1 Samuel 1:8 tell us that God remembered Hannah the second wife of Elkanah. When Elkanah found Hannah weeping, he asked her why her heart was grieved. Knowing that in days past she had been humiliated and ridiculed by Peninnah, the first wife of Elkanah who had no trouble bearing children for her husband. Hannah had reason to cry out to God for an answer as to why her womb had been closed. She knew that the path to motherhood also equated to her womanhood and being without child she felt less than. In 1 Samuel 1:11 she cried as she vowed *O Lord of hosts, if thou wilt indeed look on the affliction of thine handmaid, and remember me, and not forget thine handmaid, wilt give unto thine handmaid a man child, then I will give him unto*

the Lord all the days of his life, and there shall no razor come upon his head.*

Her prayers did not fall on deaf ears when she vowed to God, and through her prayer and supplication, would dedicate her child back to Him. God answered Hannah when she became pregnant with Samuel who became one of the greatest prophets in the history of Israel. Samuel continued to keep communication with God. And, in addition to Samuel, God gave Hannah 3 more sons and 2 daughters. 1 Sam 1:26-27 Hannah prayed

> *Oh my lord, as thy soul liveth, my lord, I am the woman that stood by thee here, praying unto the Lord. For this child I prayed, and the Lord hath given me my petition which I asked of him: Therefore also I have lent him to the Lord; as long as he liveth he shall be lent to the Lord. And he worshipped the Lord there."*

Jairus (Mark 5:22-42)

Jairus was a well-known religious leader and ruler in the synagogue of Capernaum. and father of a 12-year old daughter. According to Scripture, as Jesus was passing through Decapolis, Jairus humbled himself before Jesus by falling down at His feet as he pleaded with Jesus to come lay hands on his only daughter who was near death. Mark 5:23 says he prayed right in front of everyone,

> *My little daughter lieth at the point of death: I pray thee, come and lay thy hands on her, that she may be healed, and she shall live.*

As Jesus went with Jairus, they had to make their way through the pressing crowd. As they pressed their way, Scripture says a certain woman who had suffered with an issue of blood for twelve years, came up behind Jesus and touched the hem of his garment. In Mark 5:27, the woman who was not identified by name said in Verse 28. *If I may touch but his clothes, I shall be whole.* Her flow of blood dried up immediately. Jesus felt the virtue had gone out of him and asked *(30) Who touched my clothes?"* The woman fell down before him and told him the truth. Jesus said to her *(34) Daughter, thy faith hath made thee whole: go in peace and be whole of thy plague.*

Meanwhile, by the time Jesus and Jairus continued onto the house, they were met with weeping mourners who said the girl was dead. When Jesus came in Mark 5:39 says he saith unto them, *(39) Why make ye this ado, and weep? The damsel is not dead but sleepeth."* The mourners laughed and scorned Jesus before He put them all out. He took the father, mother and three disciples who were with him, Peter, James and John into the room. When Jesus took the girl by the hand, he spoke *(41) Damsel, I say unto thee, arise* and she arose and walked

Others that prayed and received an answer from God:

Moses (Exodus 32:11-14)

And Moses besought the Lord his God, and said, Lord, why doth thy wrath wax hot against thy people, which thou hast brought forth out of the land of Egypt with great power, and with a might hand? Wherefore should the Egyptians speak, and say. For mischief did he bring them out, to slay them in the mountains, and to consume them from the face of the earth? Turn from thy fierce wrath, and repent of this evil against thy people. Remember Abraham, Isaac, and Israel, thy servants to whom thou swarest by thine own self, and saidst unto them, "I will multiply your seed as the stars of heaven, and all this land that I have spoken of will I give unto your seed, and they shall inherit it forever. And the Lord repented of the evil which he thought to do unto his people.

Solomon (I Kings 8:22-24)
And Solomon stood before the altar of the Lord in the presence of all the congregation of Israel, and spread forth his hands toward heaven: And he said, Lord God of Israel, there is no god like thee, in heaven above, or on earth beneath, who keepest covenant and mercy with thy servants that walk before thee with all their heart: Who hast kept with thy servant David my father that thou promisedst him: thou spakest also with thy mouth, and hast fulfilled it with thine hand as it is this day.

Prayers That Jesus Prayed
Jesus (Luke 22:41-46)
The night Jesus was betrayed, he prayed to His Father, as He was alone in the Garden of Gethsemane.

And he was withdrawn from them about a stone's cast, and kneeled down, and prayed. Saying Father, if thou be willing, remove this cup from me: nevertheless not my will, but thine, be done. And there appeared an angel unto him from heaven, strengthening him. And being in an agony he prayed more earnestly: and his sweat was as it were great drops of blood falling down to the ground.

Jesus was making reference to the suffering he was about to endure. Why did he ask his Father to "let this cup pass from me?" Because he was fully human, and by nature He struggled knowing unbearable torture was imminent. He expressed wanting to avoid the human pain and suffering he was about to encounter. Along with the outward pain and suffering, He also struggled with the mental and emotional stress of wanting to fulfill the will of His Father and not His own will.

Mark 8:31 tell us that Jesus foretells of His death and resurrection.

And he began to teach them, that the Son of man must suffer many things, and be rejected of the elders, and of the chief priests, and scribes, and be killed, and after three days rise again.

Another verse depicting Jesus praying to the Father and asking if there was any other way to redeem mankind can be found in Matthews 4:12.

Neither is there salvation in any other for there is none other name under heaven given among men, whereby we must be saved.

So, then Jesus was committed to the will of God, mind, body and soul. The prayer of the righteous is always dependent on the will of God. It should be of some comfort to us, that Jesus knows what it's like to want God's will and yet not to want it. As we face conflicts, it's human nature that our flesh may often want to resist doing what's right. The conflict itself is not sinful; but it's only by practicing a sincere and prayerful life that are we able to keep our flesh under subjection which gives us the desire to walk in God's will and not our own.

An article from GotQuestions.org[12] states, "What can we learn from the prayers that Jesus prayed? Answer: The prayers Jesus prayed

---

12 GotQuestions.org

give us insight into His nature, His heart, and His mission on earth. The prayers of Jesus also inform and encourage us in our own prayer lives. Far more important than where He prayed, when He prayed, and in what position He prayed is the fact that He prayed. The theme of His prayers is instructive to all of us. Background on the basis for some of His prayers are as follows:

Prayer was an integral part of Jesus' time on earth, and He prayed regularly: "Jesus often withdrew to lonely places and prayed (Luke 5:16). If the Son incarnate found it necessary to commune with the Father frequently, how much more do we need to do so? Jesus faced persecution, trials, heartaches, and physical suffering. Without regular and continual access to the throne of God, He would surely have found those events unbearable. In the same way, Christians must never neglect to "approach God's throne of grace with confidence, so that we may receive mercy and find grace to help us in our time of need" (Hebrews 4:16)

What is often called "The Lord's Prayer" is actually a teaching tool of Christ as part of His Sermon on the Mount (Matthew 6:9-11). In this model prayer, Jesus teaches us to approach God as "our Father"; to hallow God's name; to pray for God's will; and to ask for daily provision, forgiveness, and spiritual protection.

In addition to His regular times of prayer, Jesus prayed at some important events in His life: He prayed at His baptism (Luke 3:21-22); before feeding the 5,000 (Luke 9:16) and the 4,000 (Matthew 15:36); and the moment of His transfiguration (Luke 9:29). Before Jesus chose His twelve disciples, He "spent the night praying to God" on a mountainside (Luke 6:12).

Jesus prayed at the return of the seventy-two disciples: "At the time Jesus, full of joy through the Holy Spirit, said, 'I praise you, Father, Lord of heaven and earth, because you have hidden these things from the wise and learned, and revealed them to little children. Yes, Father, for this is what you were pleased to do'" (Luke 10:21)

Jesus prayed at Lazarus' tomb. As they rolled away the stone from His friend's tomb, "Jesus looked up and said, 'Father, I thank you that you have heard me. I knew that you always hear me, but I said this for the benefit of the people standing here, that they may believe that you sent me'." (John 11:41-42). This is a good example of prayer prayed in the hearing of others for the sake of the hearers.

Jesus prayed in the Garden of Gethsemane just before His arrest (Matthew 26:36-46). He had asked His disciples to pray with Him, but they fell asleep instead. Jesus' agonized prayer in the garden is a model of submission and sacrifice: "My Father, if it is possible, may this cup be taken from me. Yet not as I will, but as you will" (verse 39). Three times Jesus prayed this.

Jesus prayed from the cross, in the midst of His agony. His first prayer echoes (Psalm 22:1) and expresses His deep distress: "About three in the afternoon Jesus cried out in a loud voice, "Eli, Eli, lama sabachthani?" (which means "My God, my God, why have you forsaken me?" (Matthew 27:46). Jesus also prayed for the forgiveness of those who were torturing Him to death: "Father, forgive them, for they do not know what they are doing" (Luke 23:34). In His final breath, Jesus continued to express His faith in God: "Father, into your hands I commit my spirit" (Luke 23:46)

Several themes are apparent in Jesus' prayers. One is the giving of thanks to the Father. Praise was a regular part of Jesus' prayers. Another theme is His communion with the Father; His relationship with His heavenly Father naturally resulted in His desire to spend time communicating with Him. The third theme in Jesus' prayers is His submission to the Father. Our Lord's prayers were always in accordance with God's will."

AND WHEN WE PRAY

There is much for us to glean from the prayers of Jesus. We can see from His prayer in the Garden of Gethsemane, that although Jesus asked God to take the cup from Him, He also expresses that it is ultimately God's will that must be accomplished. This show that Jesus knew God, His Father would not permit any prayer that is outside of His will. In Psalm 22:1 Jesus ask God "why has He forsaken Him." That scripture again shows the humanity of Jesus as he experiences what appears to be abandonment from His Father. Our purpose here on earth is to adhere to the examples of Jesus Christ, so that God our Father is as pleased with us as He is with His Son Jesus Christ.

Testimonials from Prayer Warriors

BELOW ARE TESTIMONIALS from prayer warriors that I've known to have labored and ministered in God's vineyard for many years. The purpose of this survey was to introduce each individual personality and how they approach the subject matter of prayer, and how personal prayer can be. Each testimony is based on five specific survey questions as follows:

Name: Yvonda W.
When did you volunteer or accept the call as Prayer Warrior?

I accepted the call as Prayer Warrior at an early age. I knew in my heart He (Jesus) would be my shield, strength and refuse. His love would be my guide for life. Philippians 3:3

Your view of the most important charge or responsibility of a Prayer Warrior.

My responsibility and charge as a prayer warrior would be to love God, trust Him, and be obedient always. Be ready to meet the challenge as prayer warrior with the love of God because He gave me power over fear, and my love for Him causes me to be fervent in faith for whom I'm praying for.

What strengthens you in this fight against the enemy (Satan)?
The strength to fight against Satan is to meet the challenge before me God has already given me strength of His love to shun fear, which is His love power and a sound mind. Being a doer of the Holy Word of God, which is my weapon, knowing God is with me always.

What weapons of warfare do you find most effective in getting prayers answered?
Facing the warfare for others or myself, I must be diligent and fervent in prayer. Know the Word and speaking it out.

Can you briefly cite at least two prayer requests that God has answered on your behalf?
1. Was hospitalized in my late 20's, undergoing medical research. The doctors thought they had done all the research before them. I was experiencing medical repairs concerning G.I. and abdominal issues. Possible options being surgery. I was told they had done all they knew, and they were sending me home. I presented my prayers to the Lord, asking Him to sustain me because I was a mother with younger children I needed to raise. The Lord answered my prayer; I was sent home and returned to my job.

2. In 1975, at the age of only 35 years old, I was hemorrhaging again; doctors were concerned and started preparing me for

surgery. The surgery required them to stop at that time, and they said I needed to get my system built up before they could perform the type of surgery needed to correct the problem. Doctors said they encountered some complication during the surgery. But by November of that year, and after taking my prayer request to God, He gave me sense of relief and peace at the prospect of continuing on with surgery. The surgery was performed and was successful.

AND WHEN WE PRAY

Name: Karen Y.

When did you volunteer or accept the call as Prayer Warrior?

I accepted the call as a prayer warrior after I joined LPCC about seven years ago.

Your view of the most important charge or responsibility of a Prayer Warrior.

The most important charge or responsibility of a prayer warrior is to hedge up the wall and stand in the gap to intercede before God on behalf of the land and all people, to stand with determination, persistence, faith and patience.

What strengthens you in this fight against the enemy (Satan)?

Knowledge in the Word of God and the infilling of the Holy Spirit who is the power source strengthens me in this fight against the enemy.

What weapons of warfare do you find most effective in getting prayers answered?

The most effective weapons of warfare in getting prayers answered, is praying the Word of God. His word is His will. He watches over His word to make sure they are fulfilled.

Can you briefly cite at least two prayer requests that God has answered on your behalf?

1. Prayer request answered - He supplies seed to sow for every special offering: Heavenly Father I enter your gates with thanksgiving and your courts with praise. I praise you for you are Jehovah Jireh. You are the one who sees my needs ad provides

for them. Lord your word declares that it is you who supply seeds to the sower and bread for food. You said, you would supply and multiply my seeds for sowing and increase the harvest of my righteousness. Now Father supply and multiply my seed according to the unchanging nature of your counsel so that I may be able to give generously on every occasion and my generosity will result in thanksgiving to you Lord. Lord hear my prayer and attended to my supplication in the Name of Jesus I pray. Amen

2. Prayer Request answered for open door for my daughter to attend college. Heavenly Father I enter your gates with thanksgiving and your courts with praise. I praise you for you are the God of all grace. You are the source and sustainer of all things. You sustain all things by your powerful word. Lord my children have been taught of you. And you said great shall be their peace and undisturbed composure. My daughter has walked in integrity and obedience, she has done all that she knows to do; yet she has not gotten a scholarship nor received adequate financial aid funding. Lord you said in your word that no good thing will you withhold from them that walk uprightly before you. Father raise up someone to use their power, ability and influence to help her. Open the door for her to run her race. Level every mountain and maker the crooked path straight. And let your favor surround my daughter as with a shield in the Name of Jesus I pray. Amen

Not only did God open the door, she was granted a wrestling scholarship, enrolled in a college that has one of the best Nursing Program in WA and her remaining tuition/boarding is well within her parents' budget. No stress, no strain and no struggle. To God be the glory for the things He has done!

AND WHEN WE PRAY

Name: Doneita H.

When did you volunteer or accept the call as Prayer Warrior?
Upon salvation as I believe that the call to be a prayer warrior is one that is givenby God when initiated in the Kingdom of God. However, the dimensions ofprayer accessed change through the years as an individual's prayer life matures.

Your view of the most important charge or responsibility of a Prayer Warrior.
To war until the battle is won, no matter the cost. The completion of the assignment is paramount.

What strengthens you in this fight against the enemy (Satan)?
I believe in this season our greatest most effective weapon against the enemy is our relationship with God. It is from our personal relationship with God that we access the strength needed to wield all other weapons of prayer.

What weapons of warfare do you find most effective in getting prayers answered?
My love for Christ and the desire to see his Kingdom manifested in the earth. That is mygoal as a prayer warrior to bring the things on the heart of Jesus from heaven toearth.

Can you briefly cite at least two prayer requests that God has answered on your behalf?
1. While convalescing from a broken hip, my mother developed several major blood clots in both legs. She was placed on a blood thinner by the physicians and I was informed that it would

take at least 6 months or more for resolution. After prayer utilizing the Generational Deliverance Prayer Technique, she was clot free within 4 months. This was significant in that I lost my older sister from a single blood clot originating in a broken leg over 30 years ago.

2. A family member was having difficulty at their job due to an overbearing and disrespectful boss. This maltreatment began to affect the family member's productivity causing it to decrease drastically. This resulted in the boss becoming even more overbearing and disrespectful. After performing spiritual warfare, the family member's productivity steadily increased until the individual's numbers became the highest in the company for the year.

AND WHEN WE PRAY

Name: Sis. Bettie B.

When did you volunteer or accept the call as Prayer Warrior?

As a child about 8-years old, I learned from my Pastor that praying was equivalent to talking to God. Our prayers were not supposed to be repetitious.

Your view of the most important charge or responsibility of a Prayer Warrior.

When you go to God in prayer, be sincere and have a clean heart.

What strengthens you in this fight against the enemy (Satan)?

Knowing the scripture Isaiah 54:17

No weapon that is formed against thee shall prosper; and every tongue that shall rise against thee in judgment thou shalt condemn. This is the heritage of the servants of the Lord and their righteousness is of me. Saith the Lord.

What weapons of warfare do you find most effective in getting prayers answered?

Psalm 27 and Psalm 37

Can you briefly cite at least two prayer requests that God has answered on your behalf?

1. My doctor told me it was time for a colonoscopy, so immediately when I got home; I went into prayer and asked God to get me through that procedure. Even though the light anesthesia upon starting the procedure, I could hear the doctor say, "looks like something here, maybe a polyp; but before the procedure

was over, I heard him say, "guess I was mistaken, I don't see anything here."

2. During another doctor visit, I was told that based on my lab tests, I had symptoms of Hepatitis C. My doctor referred me to a specialist who said my liver count was elevated. Between the 1st and 2nd appointments, I prayed and asked God to heal my body. I told God that he knew everything about me, and I was depending on Him. The subsequent appointment showed there was no evidence of Hep C. I was told that no treatment or medication was needed. I trust in God for everything.

AND WHEN WE PRAY

Name: Carolyn C.

When did you volunteer or accept the call as Prayer Warrior?
When I realized my capacity to intercede on other's behalf.

Your view of the most important charge or responsibility of a Prayer Warrior.
In my view, the most important responsibility of a pray warrior is to remain open to hear from God.

What strengthens you in this fight against the enemy (Satan)?
What strengthens me in this fight against the enemy is my faith, and the faithfulness of God.

What weapons of warfare do you find most effective in getting prayers answered?
The weapons of warfare I find most effective in getting prayers answered are:
1. Faith in the promises of God
2. The Word
3. Patience

Can you briefly cite at least two prayer requests that God has answered on your behalf?
1. A miraculous healing from sciatica.

2. God's protection for my children during their formative years, when some of their decisions had the propensity for destruction of their future life/welfare.

Name: Edwyna C.

When did you volunteer or accept the call as a prayer warrior?

I accepted Christ Jesus into my heart at the age of 13. I prayed for all who came to me with a need; or that I saw, by the aid of the Holy Spirit, with a need.

Your view of the most important charge or responsibility of a Prayer Warrior.

I believe the most important charge, and indeed responsibility, of a Prayer Warrior is tied to the Great Commission, Matthew 28:19-20, which tells us to spread the Gospel compelling others to come to Christ Jesus. Therefore, believers' outward show of being a prayer warrior reflects their total faith, in God. Believing that confessing with the mouth and believing in your heart does bring Salvation, is faith. Faith is that God is alive, He is omnipotent, all-powerful, He is a covenant keeper, and that God's promises are true. So, walking in our faith compels others to request our prayers in their behalf.

What strengthens you in this fight against the enemy (Satan)?

My faith in God is that God is alive, that I am God's child, as an inheritance into the family of God, He is omnipotent, all powerful, and He is a covenant keeper, God's promises are true, and His Word in Isaiah 54:17 says. "No weapon that is formed against thee shall prosper; and every tongue *that* shall rise against thee in judgment thou shalt condemn. This *is* the heritage of the servants of the Lord, and their righteousness *is* of me, saith the Lord."

AND WHEN WE PRAY

What weapons of warfare do you find most effective in getting prayers answered?

Praying the Word of God is most effective. God's Word says, In Ephesians 6:17-19. 17 ". . . take the helmet of salvation, and the sword of the Spirit, which is the word of God. 18 Praying always with all prayer and supplication in the Spirit, and watching thereunto with all perseverance and supplication for all saints; 19 And for me, that utterance may be given unto me, that I may open my mouth boldly, to make known the mystery of the gospel,"

Can you briefly sight at least two prayer requests that GOD has answered on your behalf?

1. The prayer requests I am citing is where both incidents led to my praying for God's intervention for elderly loved ones. The first incident was with my mother. I was awakened to a vision given me regarding impending danger in traffic, late one night. I learned two weeks later, that though the near interstate tragedy accident actually occurred; it was without injury to any of the people or their vehicles; but thanks to my mother calling for help from my brother. She told me of traffic incident she was involved in, and that all were safe. Only by accident did I learn my vision was an actual incident! But, I had prayed mightily on that night!

2. The other was another loved one who was going blind, was hospitalized, and she lived in another state. We, her closest relatives, lived in a different state. Again, it was late at night, and I made it a habit to call, and check on her and there was no answer, yet my spirit could not pass this feeling of uneasiness. I contacted hospitals near her home, to no avail. Finally, the

thought came to mind to ask one of our church deaconesses for the same city and state hospitals. She gave me the names of a few hospitals. I contacted the hospitals and found our dear cousin. The next day we drove to where she was, and she was in fact blind, and no one knew where she might live for proper care. However, with proper care from the doctors, we were able to take her home, where she could be comfortable, and where she remained until the Lord called her home.

Conclusion

IN SUMMARY, WE see overall, that prayer can be a powerful tool when we use it to get through difficult times. And when we use it to get those things, we desire that fall within the boundaries of God's will for us. This book gives clear and precise reasons why prayer in the life of the believer is important. We know that if our prayer is in accordance with the will of God, He will hear us, and answer us. We also know that it's up to each individual to either accept or reject God's word and His will for us. As free moral agents, we are free to live our lives according to how we see fit. But with that independence, and our own personal choices, comes consequences for the decisions we make that do not line up with God's will for us.

God has put in place a road map for us to follow; one that will lead to many blessings, and an abundance of life. These blessings however are based on our willingness to adhere to several conditions. Those conditions are given to us as commands in the scriptures. Through the scriptures, we have been given many examples of those who have prayed with amazing results as proof that God answers prayer. Prayer warriors who live by and depend on God's unfailing word, know that we fight our battles using the weapons of warfare God has given us.

AND WHEN WE PRAY

We know the practice of diligent prayer, periodic fasting, and putting on the whole armor of God brings results. We know that these weapons have been tried and tested and will cause us to prosper. We know we can effect change in our lives and often in the lives of others.

Using information from Chapter 6 on personal prayer, and the 3-step instructions above, you can start building and recording your own personal prayers. Along with lined sheets at the back of this book, I have provided some names of God, Jesus Christ, and the Holy Spirit. These scriptures reference how those names were given and why and may assist you in formulating your prayer.

To further cement your knowledge and understanding of all the information that been disseminated through this book, a workbook is being provided.

About the Author

DR. PHYLLIS GLASS is an author of three books and a minister at Living Praise Christian Church for the Mature Adult Ministry in Palmdale, California. An ordained minister of the Gospel since 1993, she has conducted workshops and seminars for work and church for more than twenty-five years. Dr. Glass is filled with the Holy Ghost and speaks and teaches under the anointing of God.

Prior to becoming an author, she retired after ten years with the California State Department of Correction as a Credentialed Business Occupations Instructor; and twenty-three years of administration and business management in the aerospace sector. Dr. Glass holds a Doctor of Divinity degree and a Bachelor of Science degree in Business Administration. She is the mother of five adult children, two sons, three daughters, four grandsons, five granddaughters, and two great-grandchildren. Dr. Glass lives in Palmdale, California.

Acknowledgments

THE PASTORS THAT have made an impact on realizing the importance of this Christian journey, whose encouragement through teaching and preaching the gospel, and the level of responsibility we bear to do the works of Him that sent us.

Dr. Rev. Johnny W. Brown, St. Timothy Community Church, SanBernardino, California

Bishop Henry Hearns, Pastor Emeritus of Living Stone Cathedral of Worship, Littlerock, California

Pastors Dr. Fred L and Linda Hodge, Living Praise Christian Church,Palmdale, California

To Willa Robinson, author and publisher of KP Publishing Company, whose encouragement throughout this process gave me great hope in being a contributor of providing meaningful work to those who otherwise may not have been connected to the Kingdom of God.

To J. P. Carter, whose outstanding gift and work in photography lends itself to the photo of this author.

Bibliography

1. Merriam Webster
2. Oxford Dictionary
3. Dakes Annotated Reference Bible, Old and New Testaments of Authorized or King James Version Text by Finis Jennings, Pages 1043-1044
4. American Heritage College Dictionary
5. Sam Storms, Pastor, Oklahoma City, OK, April 29, 2018 www.desiringgod.org/articles/seven-ays-to-quench-the-spirit
6. Dakes Annotated Reference Bible, Old and New Testaments of Authorized or King James Version Text by Finis Jennings, Page 375
7. Eric Landstrom, Ephesians 6:10-17: Spiritual Warfare and the Celestial City of God
8. Webster's New World Roget's Thesaurus
9. Linda G. Hodge, Jr., Pastor, Living Praise Christian Church
10. Dakes Annotated Reference Bible, Old and New Testaments of Authorized or King James Version Text by Finis Jennings, Pages 1043

11. Dakes Annotated Reference Bible, Old and New Testaments of Authorized or King James Version Text by Finis Jennings, Pages 346
12. GotQuestions.org
http://www.gotquestions.org/about.html

Other Books by Dr. Phyllis Glass

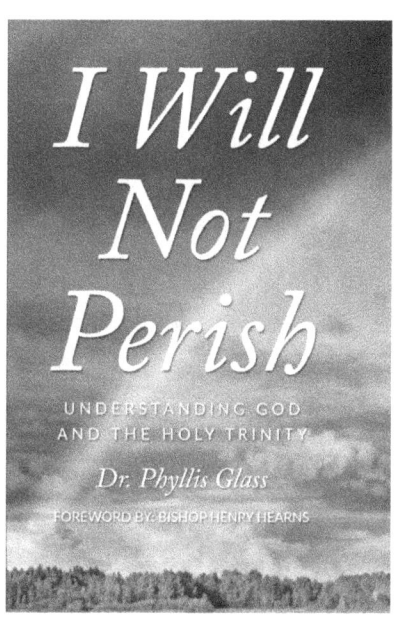

www.ingramcontent.com/pod-product-compliance
Lightning Source LLC
Chambersburg PA
CBHW072039110526
44592CB00012B/1485